Good Housekeeping

the full facts

without the fuss

+ practical advice

and recipes

Organic handbook

HarperCollins*Illustrated*

First published in 2001 by HarperCollins*Illustrated*
an imprint of HarperCollins*Publishers*
77-85 Fulham Palace Road
London W6 8JB

The HarperCollins website address is:
www.**fire**and**water**.com

Published in association with
The National Magazine Company Limited
Good Housekeeping is a registered trade mark of
The National Magazine Company Limited

The Good Housekeeping website address is
www.goodhousekeeping.co.uk

A CIP catalogue record for this book is available
from the British Library

ISBN: 0 00 711689 6

Colour reproduction by Saxon Photolitho
Printed and bound in Hong Kong by Printing Express

This book is typeset in Helvetica and HelveticaNeue

contents

foreword

When I was a child, the word organic was never mentioned. People would buy their fruit, vegetables and eggs from one shop (the supply came from local farms) and meat from the local butcher. Then the fish man would drop by once a week selling the catch of the day. Everything was fresh, local produce and we all knew where it came from.

Over the past decade we've had numerous food scares to contend with – from salmonella and BSE to the use of antibiotics in farming and genetic modification. It's hardly surprising, then, that when it comes to knowing what is and isn't safe to eat, some of us can be thrown into a state of panic and confusion.

But there's still so much to celebrate about our food, and the good news is that organics is the food industry's fastest growing area. Supermarkets currently stock an average of 1000 organic lines and their sales account for around 70 per cent of organic produce bought. Organic box delivery schemes and farmers markets are on the increase, too: there are now around 300 across the country. Yes, organic food is more expensive than mass-produced but you can be sure it has been grown to exacting standards and without the routine use of pesticides or artificial fertilisers.

But 'organic' isn't just about the food we eat, it's also about they way we live: our wellbeing, the energy used in our homes, how we garden, and safeguarding both our and our children's future.

This book is a brilliant reference guide to how we can adjust our daily habits in order to make all our lives better in the long run. Good Housekeeping regularly campaigns for improvements in all areas of our lives – be it relating to food or consumer issues or health and homes.

So whether you're doing your weekly shop, buying a new appliance, decorating your home or doing up your garden, this book will provide all the practical, straightforward advice you'll need to help you take a part in improving your life. Enjoy!

Aggie MacKenzie
Associate Editor
Good Housekeeping Institute

why
organic?

Choosing the best food from the vast bounty that is available to us in this new century is one of the most important things we can do to enrich our lives and nourish those who sit at our table. By choosing organic produce we provide food that is wholesome to eat and a positive benefit to health as it is free from disease and chemical residues. The choice also helps to protect the planet on which we all depend because organic methods of food production are truly sustainable: food is grown in traditional ways that help protect fragile eco-systems and enrich the soil in which it is grown. Now is the time for a positive change.

organic food production

Organic farming uses methods as old as agriculture itself. Today these practices of keeping the earth healthy with natural fertilizers and rotating crops still protect the soil from exhaustion and encourage wildlife to help keep pests at bay. The wider the diversity of species, the healthier the plants and the more resistant they are to disease. Good animal husbandry helps to safeguard those raised for food from stress and ill health.

Buying organic

When we buy food that is certified and labelled 'organic' it is produced by methods defined by a strict set of laws. Organic farmers avoid the use of artificial chemical fertilizers and pesticides; this allows micro-organisms and earthworms to keep the soil in prime condition for growing, and allows natural predators of crop pests to flourish. Animals are reared without the routine use of drugs such as antibiotics and growth promoters. All organic produce contains far fewer potentially dangerous residues that could affect your health and the environment.

Green plants require some sixteen different elements to grow, which they have to find in the soil, plus carbon and hydrogen dioxide from the atmosphere. Three of the most critical for adequate plant nutrition are nitrogen, phosphorus and potassium. Phosphorus can be obtained from rock or bones, potassium from potash deposits, and nitrogen from the naturally occurring substance saltpetre or potassium nitrate and from the atmosphere, as well as from plants such as beans and clover. Ancient civilizations used fertilizers such as ground bones, wood ash, dried blood, bird droppings and fish to boost the elements in the soil. The Romans discovered that adding lime to the soil made acid soil productive and that beans could take nitrogen from the air and convert it into a form that plant roots could access; Latin texts describe the advantages of crop rotation.

In order for soil to replenish itself naturally it needs to be fertilized with natural materials and a diversity of crops need to be planted in rotation, as different crops take different levels of specific elements from the soil. Organic farmers are required to alternate crops so that they do not always grow in the same place; this maintains the health of the ground and does not encourage the build-up of soil-borne disease and pests.

Changes in practice

The Second World War led to shortages of many foods, and increased yields due to artificial fertilizers may have kept people from starvation during the war; but when meat, fat and sugar consumption were rationed the general standard of health improved. When rationing was finally lifted there was a clamour for more and more comfort food in the form of just those restricted items. The emergence of intensive animal rearing, where cattle and poultry were reared indoors and fed on artificial supplements and growth promoters seemed to provide the dream of cheap and widely available convenience foods. At that stage few people worried about the chemicals that were used. It was novel, lavishly promoted by advertising, readily available and cheap. This was the food of a brave new world.

Organic pioneers

There were a few dissenting voices. During the War, even though it was deemed unpatriotic to suggest that intensive methods of production might be dangerous, in 1943 Lady Eve Balfour published *The Living Soil*. In it she wrote that 'only by faithfully returning to the soil in due course everything that has come from it can fertility be made permanent and the earth be helped ... starting with a truly fertile soil, the crops grown on it, the livestock fed on those crops, and the humans fed on both, have a standard of health and a power of resisting disease'.

Eve Balfour was one of the first to state the problems with intensive farming, and fortunately nowadays the tide is turning back in favour of more sustainable methods of

production. During the last fifty years there have been alarming increases in allergies, food sensitivities, asthma, coronary heart disease, diabetes and cancers. These are in part due to pollution but undoubtedly also to do with the extreme change to our diet and way of life. By adopting an organic lifestyle and eating organic food, we should be able to avoid or alleviate many health and environmental problems.

Problems with intensive farming

For millennia all food was produced organically, and in many less developed countries this is still the case, but in the developed world the twentieth century saw a drive for increased agricultural production, which heralded the rise of chemical fertilizers, herbicides and pesticides.

The German chemist Fritz Haber won the Nobel Prize in 1918 for his discovery of a method of synthesizing ammonia. Together with his colleague Carl Bosch, he invented a process of manufacturing ammonia for use in nitrogen fertilizer, an important discovery because stocks of the natural source were drying up. These artificial fertilizers allowed farmers to increase their yields and they were encouraged to use them both to produce food that was cheap and to use them as substitutes for the traditional practices of rotation and diversity – to plant instead, monocrops of high-yielding cereals, for example, year after year.

Unfortunately, synthesized nitrogen fertilizer does not enrich the soil and has to be constantly reapplied. In addition, it is often washed off by rainfall before it has had a chance to be absorbed by the plants. If excessive nitrogen runs off into a body of water, it can reduce the dissolved oxygen in the water in ponds, streams, rivers and lakes. This allows algae and other water plants to proliferate and choke forms of life such as fish and other organisms that live in the water.

When a farmer plants the same crop year after year, he needs to doctor his depleted soil with chemicals in order for anything to grow at all, as the soil will not itself contain the nutrition that plants need. This provides a perfect opportunity for destructive organisms to increase and multiply. If the crop they feed on is not there these organisms cannot thrive, which is why rotation is such a vital part of good farming practice. Simply, animals and plants that are reared and grown with the constant application of chemicals are weak and vulnerable to diseases and infections.

Eco-friendly techniques

The UK Office of National Statistics reported that food poisoning in the UK increased six-fold between 1985 and 2000, at the cost of several billion pounds every year. One of the reasons given was 'more intensive rearing of chickens and farm animals under conditions that can spread germs'.

● Unhygienic conditions in intensive rearing systems have proved to be a perfect breeding ground for dangerous organisms in food derived from animals
● Intensive factory farming is the perfect breeding ground for infective agents, such as salmonella in chickens, which are an extremely serious threat to our health
● Roughly half of the poultry and many of the raw meat products, such as beefburgers and pork sausages, on sale from intensive farms are infected with salmonella, campylobacter and *E. coli* – the agents responsible for most outbreaks of food poisoning
● Many animals are already infected before they arrive at the abattoir but pathogens can also enter the food chain by improper handling of carcasses contaminated during slaughter and processing
● According to the World Health Organization more than half of the world's total production of antimicrobial antibiotic drugs is currently used on farm animals – with much of it being given not to treat disease but to promote growth. This encourages the emergence and persistence of resistant strains of infections such as salmonella
● Growth-promoting antibiotics can actually increase animals' susceptibility and may be creating a build-up of bacteria resistant to medicines given to humans
● The misuse of antibiotics is killing off the naturally present good bacteria, which help to control disease-causing pathogens
● Substances such as clenbuterol or 'angel dust' are often misused to increase the amount of muscle in farm animals. This can cause increased heart rate and heart tremors in both humans and animals
● Growth-promoting hormones such as trenbolone and various steroid hormones have been linked to melanoma; these have been banned by the EU since 1988 but a number of countries, including the US, are working to have the ban lifted
● Anabolic hormones are used in the US, Canada and Australia to allow cattle to put on weight after castration. These steroids can cause bone, liver and other abnormalities in the animals and may have serious consequences for human health

why organic?

the benefits

We are what we eat. By supporting the organic movement we choose not only to feed ourselves with what is best for our health but also to help to protect and support the myriad other life forms with which we share our earth. What we put into our shopping baskets and on to our plates does matter. Consumers *do* have power. We vote with our money. Market demand is ultimately not about what producers and multinational corporations choose to offer, but what we are actually willing to buy.

In everyone's interest

All farmers are entitled to make a decent living and we all need to be able to buy wholesome food at a reasonable cost. It is in all our interests to ensure that we don't unwittingly pay too high a price for cheap food that can threaten not only our survival but could also destroy our environment beyond repair. The methods used by organic farmers – careful animal husbandry, tried-and-true methods of crop rotation and seasonal planting, combined with the restricted use of chemicals – help to protect biodiversity. This is one of the most important benefits of organic farming, in addition to providing us with food that is safe and healthy to eat.

Why is biodiversity important?

We need as wide a range of wildlife and plants as possible to ensure the health of consumers as well as the health of the planet. When we lose plants and the wild creatures that depend on them or pollinate them we lose potential sources of food and energy for the future, so we narrow the range of human possibilities. Once a plant or animal has become extinct, it can never be brought back.

In the name of farming, humans have changed the landscape to such a degree during the past fifty years that the world's vegetation and wildlife are threatened. Intensive chemical-based farming typically relies on growing monocultures of one crop, or raising herds of one type of animal, or reseeding meadows and pastures with monocultures of nitrogen-hungry grasses. This destroys naturally diverse habitats, depletes the soil and encourages the spread of disease. It also forces into extinction a wide variety of useful plants and creatures.

The aim of organic farmers is to protect the fragile balance of crops, pests and predators. Birds feed on insects; spiders and other bugs feed on agricultural pests. Aphids, for example, are the favourite food of lacewing larvae, which they devour in prodigious quantities. There are many more of these beneficial birds and insects on organic farms where there is no routine spraying of insecticides to kill them off. In addition, artificial herbicides and synthetic pesticides can leach into ditches and pollute ground water, and some eventually make their way into the water we drink. Micro-organisms present in the soil cannot degrade many of the pesticides used fast enough to prevent soil and water pollution.

The benefits of encouraging a wide range of species is not restricted to bird and insect life. Ensuring the survival of the largest number of species of food plants is critical and is also of value to the farmer in terms of crop yield. If one variety were to be wiped out by disease it would be a disaster if there were no alternatives with which to replace it. It also makes sense economically. Recent research has proved that farmers who grow a wide range of plants are better off than those who are reliant on one or just a few varieties. Small farms in the US growing a wide variety of crops can be ten times more profitable per acre than vast tracts planted with one.

There is a widespread myth that it is necessary to farm intensively with agri-chemicals for farmers to make a profit. Yet harvests of organic maize have been shown to be identical to those of maize grown with fertilizers and pesticides, but the soil quality in areas where the organic maize was grown had improved dramatically. Wheat fertilized with manure has been found to produce higher yields than that fed with artificial nutrients. Similar results have been reported from all over the world.

International organics

Cuban farmers who were forced into organic farming because of an economic blockade that prevented them from buying artificial fertilizer, chemical pest controls and expensive 'improved' seeds must have been delighted at the irony when both quality and productivity improved! Farmers in India, encouraged to be 'modern' and switch from traditional methods to intensive cultivation discovered that these new crops required far more water and nutrients, resulting in a loss of ground water and depleted soil. In Brazil, Guatemala, Honduras, India and Kenya yields have been doubled and tripled by using organic and partly organic techniques.

A recent study in China compared traditional and modern methods of rice growing – a single high-tech variety in a large area compared with the traditional practice of growing several breeds together in one field. The results astonished everyone. Rice blast is a devastating fungus that normally needs continual applications of fungicide to control one intensively grown strain. In the mixed planting fields rice blast was decreased by 94 per cent, allowing the farmers to give up pesticides completely, and the yield was 18 per cent higher per acre.

More wildlife on organic farms

Other recent studies comparing the biodiversity of organic farms with farms where artificial fertilizers, pesticides and other chemicals are routinely used has shown that there are five times as many wild plants in arable fields on those farms that are managed organically, amounting to fifty-seven more species. Many rare wild species are found only on organic farms.

As well as there being a wider range of plants on organically managed farms there are reported to be up to twice as many birds on organic farms, around field edges and in the fields. This is because less pesticides result in a proliferation of insects on which the birds feed. Farming organically also provides a safe habitat for butterflies where crops are grown, and organic farms are reckoned to have up to five times as many spiders and many more species of insects than other farms, but a significant decline in the numbers of aphids.

Hospitable habitat

Many cereal crops are planted in the autumn on land that is intensively farmed, whereas organic farmers stick to the tradition of sowing in spring. This provides an ideal place for ground-nesting birds, which breed in summer and feed on the weeds and seeds in the winter stubble when other food is scarce.

It is not only the areas where crops are grown that are protected by organic standards but field margins, hedges and trees, too. Hedgerows are home to much of our disappearing wildlife – including the tiny dormouse, which is now extinct in seven counties in the UK. Organic hedgerows are larger and are cut back only at times of the year when there is minimal threat to wildlife. Some farmers encourage wildlife further by leaving a bare patch in the middle of fields where crops are growing.

European fauna and flora

The natural vegetation and wildlife in Europe have changed more drastically in the last fifty years than in preceding millennia. Numerous species of wild delphinium and campanula, for example, once common in southern Europe, are now only found in 'heirloom' flower catalogues. Varieties of once common vegetables have succumbed to the same fate as a much more limited range of modern hybrid seeds are bred for uniformity, yield, ease of harvesting and storage. Many varieties of orchids have all but disappeared from sites throughout Europe with change of land use, overgrazing, and spread of chemicals.

The demise in the UK of the large blue butterfly, extinct since 1979, was due to the destruction of grassland and overgrazing. Although the large white butterfly is regarded as a serious pest, pesticides don't make the distinction between harmful and benign species. There were almost four million skylarks in the UK in 1972, but only one and a half million are now left. This has been the greatest decline of any farmland bird, but the numbers of grey partridge, tree sparrow, bullfinch, stone curlew and song thrush are also rapidly declining. There has been no sighting of a horned dung beetle since the 1950s, and there is only one spot left in the country where the orchid, the lady's slipper *Cypripedium calceolus*, still grows.

why organic?

Who profits?

It is useful to consider just who it is that advises farmers to plant single crops and use enormous quantities of chemicals to fertilize and kill off pests. Certainly, manufacturers of agricultural chemicals have a vested interest in promoting their products. The more you use the more you need, and for the past decade major agri-chemical companies have been systematically buying up seed companies and seed-breeding laboratories. This means that farmers are encouraged to purchase the specific varieties of seed that are not killed by the selective pesticides or herbicides the same company also produces. It seems very likely that such marketing is less from any altruistic desire to feed the world but more from the motive of profit.

Organic farmers and consumers profit

The growing market for organic produce should mean that more and more farmers will profit by going organic. Consumers must recognize that it is worth paying a little extra for organic produce, considering the wide range of benefits that organic farming has to offer.

certification

'Organic' is a legal definition. Only certified organic produce can be labelled as such. Producers are governed by strict rules and subject to regular inspections. Every country has its own set of regulations and many claim that UK standards are among the highest in the world.

Basic standards

In the UK, the government body that sets the basic standards is the independent UK Register of Organic Food Standards (UKROFS). Any serious infringement of their strict regulations will result in the producer or processor having his licence suspended and his products withdrawn from the market.

Manufacturers and processors who use organic ingredients and the farmers who grow them pay an annual fee and must keep detailed records. This ensures that there is a clear path, following food from the farm to our tables.

Organics in Europe and further abroad

While each European country has its own national certification authority, it must also conform to EU standards laid down by the International Federation of Organic Agricultural Movements.

Some organic food is imported from countries outside the EU. There is some controversy as to whether or not these countries apply the same rigorous standards. Importers themselves can apply for inspection by EU-recognized certification bodies for specific organic producers whose goods they wish to sell.

UK certification
Each UK certifying body has its own symbol and an EU-assigned number.

- UKROFS (UK1) funded by the Ministry of Agriculture Fisheries and Food (MAFF) approves and supervises the other certification bodies
- Organic Farmers and Growers Ltd (UK2) is the second largest organic certification body in the UK

- Scotland has the Scottish Organic Producers Association (UK3), which conforms to UKROFS requirements
- The Organic Food Federation (UK4) is primarily a trade federation of importers, manufacturers and producers
- The symbol seen on about 70 per cent of organic food in the UK is that of the Soil Association (UK5). Its standards are said to be generally stricter and more specific than those of UKROFS

- Growers and manufacturers who conform to the Biodynamic Agricultural Association (Demeter) standards employ homeopathic and herbal preparations to treat soil, plants, compost and manure and plant at specific times of the lunar calendar (UK6)
- Irish Organic Farmers and Growers (UK7) conforms to UKROFS and their own additional standards

Organic food and GMOs

GMOs or GEs are genetically modified or genetically engineered organisms. Genetic material from one species can now be inserted into another to create a new plant. The aim may be to keep it fresher longer, make it disease, antibiotic or pesticide resistant, or to change its structure nutritionally.

● Organic food should never contain GMOs

● In one of the earliest GM experiments a protein gene from the brazil nut was put into soya beans to increase their protein content. As well as the protein from the brazil nut, the genetic material also passed on allergens that cause severe nut allergy, and the brazil nut-modified soya bean had to be scrapped

● A gene from an Arctic flounder in GM tomatoes and strawberries keeps them firm for longer than ordinary fruit

● Antibiotic resistance has been engineered in soya and maize and one-third of the US soya and 20 per cent in Argentina is now genetically modified

● In Canada, a 'superfish' has been developed by genetically modifying salmon for farming with a flounder gene. It grows six times faster and twice as big as ordinary salmon. There are more than 100,000 of these superfish and it has been calculated that it will take only forty generations for the original species to become extinct if the genetically modified fish mate with wild salmon

Organic shops and Fair Trade

Shops, too, can apply and pay a certification fee to register as 'organic', and are subject to the same strict rules and inspections. Any food that is packaged or cooked and labelled 'organic' must be licensed. When buying organic produce from other countries, look for 'Fair Trade' as well as organic labelling. These are groups who encourage more equitable and sustainable systems of production to promote 'economic, social and environmental justice worldwide'. Many items are produced by local cooperatives; workers are fairly paid and many of these Fair Trade groups reinvest in community projects such as health clinics, education and literacy projects, and in environmental programmes such as reforestation.

pesticides – do we need them?

Even though yields may be higher with the use of pesticides, the amount lost is also greater. In 1945, US farmers used about 3 per cent of the chemical pesticides they use now and pests and disease accounted for a loss of around 31 per cent of the total harvest. Today it is 37 per cent. Is this tiny rise in percentage worth the risk to the health of ourselves and the environment?

Toxic rain

A recent Swiss study found that rainwater can contain toxic levels of crop sprays. It seems these chemicals evaporated from sprayed fields to end up in clouds. It was previously assumed that pesticides only entered ground water from the soil, but the highest concentrations in rainwater occurred in the first rain after a long dry spell when nearby fields had been recently treated. Rainwater is often diverted to underground water supplies and drinking water is not ordinarily treated to remove herbicides and pesticides.

Super bugs

When the plant pests become resistant to the chemicals being used they pass it on to the next generations. They reproduce and mutate rapidly, and are programmed to adapt to survive. When most of their natural predators have been wiped out, new bugs, not previously a threat, rush to fill the vacuum and create a new 'secondary pest' problem. A study in California revealed that of the twenty-five most common, serious insect crop pests, all but one were secondary pests and seventeen were resistant to insecticides.

Pesticides and cancer risk

There is ongoing research worldwide into examining the links between agri-chemicals and human diseases.

- Research scientists in Sweden have linked several of the most commonly used crop sprays and garden pesticides to Non-Hodgkin's lymphoma, a cancer described as one of the most rapidly increasing in the Western world – up by 73 per cent in the US since 1973
- Swedish patients suffering from this disease have been shown to be almost three times more likely to have been exposed to a weed killer known as MCP (Target) widely used on grain crops
- They were also shown to have been more likely to have had contact with glyphosate-based Round-up, the most common herbicide used in Sweden
- A recent study reported in an international medical journal that people regularly exposed to pesticides are more liable to develop mild cognitive dysfunction, or memory loss, in later life. This often leads to full-blown dementia

Organic methods of pest control

Given that chemical pesticides do not always work, many ordinary farmers as well as organic growers have developed other methods to control pests. Integrated pest management (IPM) is a method that combines an array of safe methods to control pests. It uses helpful bugs such as lacewings to destroy destructive pests, and relies on biological weapons such as companion planting and the introduction of predator species, as well as botanical pesticides. Plant breeders are working to develop plants that are resistant to pests and viruses, without resorting to GMOs. The more organic produce that we consumers buy, the greater will be the incentive for conventional farmers to convert to organic farming.

food additives

Organic processed foods contain no artificial flavourings and colourings. There are strict regulations determining what can legally be added to any of the food we eat, to enhance its flavour, change its colour or texture, retard spoiling or simply make it easier to manufacture. Laws on food labelling now require manufacturers to list all of the ingredients added to prepared foods.

Small print

Many people are sensitive to even minute quantities of chemical residues, colourings and flavourings. A careful shopper can find out what has been added to prepared food by reading the small print on the label. There are excellent books that list the E-numbers assigned by the EU to permitted additives, describing what they are and if there are any health risks associated with them. Food labelling is much more informative than it used to be, with useful nutritional information provided, for example the fat, salt and sugar content. But food additives are not food, they have no nutritional value and many can be a danger to health.

Food additives may be referred to on the label by their chemical name, for example MSG (monosodium gluta-mate), or their assigned E-number. Numbers E100–180 are colouring agents, E200–290 preservatives, E300–322 antioxidants (which help to keep food from spoiling), E400–495 emulsifiers and stabilizers, to thicken the texture, and E420–421 sweeteners. Most manufacturers now list the additives by their chemical name rather than E-number.

Colouring agents are the additives most of us would consider as the least necessary since they are purely cosmetic. They are also the additives most people are sensitive to. We have all become accustomed to consuming a large quantity of unnaturally, brightly coloured foods – particularly sweets, but also juices, cereals, cakes and biscuits and even crisps, cheeses and fish. Unfortunately, many of the highly coloured items on sale are aimed at children and often promoted as suitable for children's snacks or 'perfect for school lunch boxes'.

A recent survey by The Food Commission of 358 foods aimed at children revealed that not only were many of them extremely high in sugar, saturated fat and salt, but 38 per cent had added colourings, 57 per cent added flavourings, and 68 per cent had both. One-fifth had five or more different colours and one dessert had nine different artificial hues. The yellow colouring tartrazine E102 is the most commonly reported to cause adverse reactions. It is also worth noting that the colour listed as E173 is aluminium, which may be linked to Alzheimer's disease; it is used on the external coating of confectionery and in a few liqueurs. Sulfating chemicals such as sulfur dioxide, sodium bisulfite and potassium metasulfite are used on dried fruit to keep its colour. They are not necessary to preserve it as the drying process does that. They are frequently used in dehydrated soup mixes, seafoods and syrups, and are especially hazardous to asthmatics.

Artificial sweeteners are cheaper than sugar and are used extensively in processed food and are even added to toothpaste and vitamin pills. Aspartame E951 is one of the most controversial, and the most common, and should be avoided by anyone suffering from phenylketonuria (PKU). One out of 20,000 babies is born without the ability to metabolise phenylalanine, one of the two amino acids in aspartame. It is widely used because it does not have the unpleasant aftertaste that saccharin E954 does, and saccharin is banned by the EU for use in foods meant for children up to three years old. To be safe, no sweeteners should be given to infants or young children or eaten during pregnancy. These additives may be regarded as safe to eat but they are not necessary. Wholesome, natural food contains all the colouring and flavour it needs to whet the appetite.

E-numbers

Some of the food additives assigned E-numbers have been linked to health problems, such as asthma and allergies.

Colouring agents:	E100–180
Preservatives:	E200–290
Antioxidants:	E300–322
Emulsifiers and stabilizers:	E400–495
Sweeteners:	E420–421

buying
organic

It is becoming increasingly easy to buy organic food. Some lucky shoppers already have a store nearby that sells nothing but organic produce – perhaps in the near future we all will. Supermarkets and other stores offer a wide variety of organic fare, and an expanding number of producers' outlets offer the freshest produce of all – meats, cheeses, fruit and vegetables.

Fresh from the farm

Fresh produce degrades very quickly with a loss of nutrients and flavour. If you have the opportunity, buy from a farmers' market or farm shop – some farm shops sell both local produce and imported items such as citrus and other tropical fruits to accommodate customers who are used to one-stop shopping. Organic farmers are proud of what they sell and want their customers to be more than just satisfied, and many find that personal contact with their customers results in useful feed-back and enables them to develop the kind of value-added products their customers want.

Box schemes

There are a number of ways to find out about home delivery; most organic shops and many farmers have box schemes, which means a regular delivery to your door of selected seasonal produce that is fresher than anything in a supermarket. The choice can be a little more limited and more seasonal than you are accustomed to, but if you dislike something in one box, ask for a substitute. Suppliers want their customers to be satisfied.

Fewer food miles

Every time someone touches the food you buy it adds to the cost. Buying directly from the producer makes good sense because it usually costs less and is far, far fresher. The more organic food that is produced locally the less will be imported from other countries, which may not have the same high standards that farmers closer to home do.

Buying tips

The only way to buy really fresh food is to shop often. There was a time when most people shopped daily and only bought what they could carry home in a basket – enough to last for a day or two. Small independent bakers, butchers, greengrocers and delicatessens still offer a service many customers appreciate. Open-air markets flourish in many towns and cities. Supermarkets are certainly convenient for people with busy working lives, but smaller shops will stay open later if there is enough demand from working people who find it difficult to shop during office hours.

Keep the small shops open

Supermarkets offer an increasingly good range of organic produce but they cannot compare when it comes to fresh produce. Theirs is trucked from all over the country to a central warehouse and then sent out again to individual stores. This isn't important with exotics such as bananas, which are picked green a long way away, but it does matter when, with a little effort, you could support small shops and markets and have food grown locally, which can be picked and on your plate within a day.

Only cosmetic

One of the most common criticisms aimed at organic produce is that it looks less appealing than packaged non-organic food. But looks aren't everything and one of the best ways to choose fresh produce is to smell it. If it doesn't smell of much it won't taste of much either and you can't smell anything under a layer of plastic. Besides, in their natural state, fruit and vegetables are not perfectly formed and uniform in size. It adds to the cost to sort and package those that are.

Naturally smooth and shining

All fresh food looks plump and smooth when it is fresh. One of the first things that happens when fruit and vegetables are picked is that they begin to lose water, a process that continues as they age. Leave the wrinkly ones behind and keep fresh produce dry and cool until you are ready to use it. Buy meat and fish that you can see and judge for yourself, rather than prewrapped food, which is more difficult to examine carefully.

eating and drinking

To provide the best possible sustenance for those we cherish is a universal human desire. By choosing from the ever-widening range of organically grown foods available we select what has been produced with care and concern. Everything we consume comes from the earth and it is vital for our health and well-being that this earth and all that it produces should be nurtured. The aim of every organic farmer is to send out to the market-place food of only the very highest quality by treating the land, the growing crops and the animals in their charge with respect.

drink

Beverages play an important role in our daily lives and almost everything we drink is now available in an organic version. Start the day with a cup of hot organic tea or coffee with organic milk, have a glass of organic fruit juice with breakfast, then take a break later in the day with a cup of one of the many organic herbal teas now on offer, or indulge in organic drinking chocolate. The close of a busy day can be celebrated by raising a relaxing glass of organic wine, spirit, beer or cider. There are even organic sparkling wines and champagnes to mark extra special occasions.

Drinking liquids throughout the day is not only pleasurable but a necessity. Our brains cannot function properly and we lose concentration when we are thirsty. Children in many schools are now encouraged to drink water at their desks to avoid dehydration which makes them less attentive.

Many of the fluids we drink, such as milk and fruit juice, are also a valuable source of nutrients. Organic milk is now widely available and more healthy, particularly for allergy-sufferers, because organic dairy cows are not treated with hormones and other substances to increase their milk production. Nourishing hot drinks are comforting and healing when someone is not feeling their best, and on a hot day nothing is more welcome than a long, cool glass of iced water with a splash of something to flavour it - a squeeze of lemon or other citrus fruit, or a sprig of an organically-grown herb makes plain water into something special.

fruit drinks and water

Fruit juices are a concentrated source of sugar as well as valuable vitamins and minerals such as vitamin C and folic acid. Organic juices contain no additives or preservatives, but it is still generally better for childrens' teeth if they are diluted with water, by about half or one-third.

Bottled drinks

Many bottled drinks on sale are full of sugar substitutes and artificial colourings and flavourings but the organic varieties are not. They are a better choice for any children and adults who are sensitive to even minute traces of additives, and are recommended for children with any tendency to hyperactivity which may be caused or worsened by consuming additives in food and drinks.

Juicers

Freshly juiced organic fruit and vegetables are a good way of increasing the daily intake of nutritious fruit and vegetables. A glass of juice made from an apple, a carrot and a beetroot, for example, adds up to three of the recommended 'five-a-day' servings of fresh fruit and vegetables.

Water

We all need water for our bodies to function properly. Ideally, adults should drink around 2 litres (3½ pints) a day, taken in small amounts regularly throughout the day. Drinks made with water such as tea and coffee are additional – don't include them as part of the ideal daily water intake.

Bottled waters

Tap water is safe for us to drink because the supply of household water is a highly regulated industry. However, many people prefer to drink filtered or bottled water, either because they like the taste or for health reasons. Bottled water is extremely handy when you are on the move, but once the seal on the bottle has been broken the water should be consumed as quickly as possible to avoid contamination by bacteria. If more than one person is going to be drinking from the bottle do not let anyone drink directly from it.

All bottled waters must now satisfy strict safety standards, and false or misleading claims are not allowed by law. Mineral waters contain naturally occurring minerals, which have passed into the water as it flows through various layers of earth and rock to wells or springs. The minerals should all be listed on the label. Spring water flows naturally from an underground spring with no drilling or pumping. Sparkling waters are carbonated with naturally occurring carbon dioxide. In some cases it has been taken out of the original water and put back in again for bottling. Water in a bottle that is simply called 'table water' is often ordinary water from a tap, bottled and sold at hundreds of times the price it costs to produce.

Should we filter?

It is not strictly necessary to filter tap water but many people like to, as it almost always looks clearer and tastes fresher than unfiltered. The easiest filters to use and the cheapest are jugs with replaceable filters containing charcoal, which removes bacteria and some chemicals. Remember to change the filters regularly.

If you dislike the taste and suspect the quality of your tap water it may be worth investing in a permanent filter plumbed under the kitchen sink to remove chemicals, heavy metals and bacteria. An optional additional element removes nitrates that can enter the water supply if there is agricultural run-off nearby. Install a water meter so that you can change the cartridges according to the volume of water treated rather than relying on a recommended time limit as every household uses different amounts of water.

Another option is reverse osmosis, whereby water is passed under pressure through a porous membrane, which separates the water from the other elements it contains. These guarantee the purest water and are particularly recommended where occupants of a house suffer from allergies, but the cost of installation is greater than other systems. Water softeners are not filters, they are designed to remove calcium and magnesium but not contaminants, and softened water is high in sodium chloride (salt).

alcoholic drinks

As with other organic products, wines, spirits, beers and ciders that bear the organic label are produced with minimum damage to the environment by using fewer pesticides and other chemicals. Biodiversity is encouraged and the best tried-and-true traditional methods of agriculture are used. This results in products with a fuller flavour and a fresher taste.

Supply and demand

The process of gaining organic certification requires such a strong commitment on the part of the manufacturer that organic alcoholic drinks are usually made with the greatest of care at every stage of production, and they do taste excellent. The increase in demand for everything organic has meant that drinks are becoming increasingly competitively priced; but in any case it is always worth paying a little more as the quality of most organic alcoholic drinks is simply incomparable.

Organic ciders, perrys and beers are never bland as they are often made with old, traditional varieties of apples and hops that are in danger of disappearing from the landscape, and which have been chosen for their flavour, which is the primary concern rather than high yield. So when you buy organic drinks you are not only giving yourself a healthy treat but also helping to preserve traditional varieties and rural practices that might otherwise be lost.

Labelling

Wines, beers and spirits that are labelled 'organic' have to conform to standards set by the individual countries where they are produced. These vary but generally all of the ingredients used in their production will have been grown organically, with restricted use of pesticides, fertilizers and additives, which means that there is very little risk that sprays and systemic treatments end up as residues in the final product. Organic growers must be able to prove how and where the fruits were grown, and increasingly efficient labelling means that we may soon be able to trace every organic product back to its source. This is already common practice for much organic produce where every item that goes for sale or processing has the equivalent of its own passport barcoded on to its box.

Additives

In addition to the excellent taste and quality, many wine drinkers find that organic wine is less likely to leave them with a hangover as it contains fewer chemicals. Many inexpensive wines, on the other hand, have been treated with a variety of additives and contain residues that are likely to have an adverse effect with even moderate consumption. It is rarely the wine that gives you a head-ache, but the chemicals in it.

In Europe, a wine that is made only from organically grown grapes can be called organic, but in the US 'organic' can mean wine bottled without preservatives – even if the grapes have been grown with chemical inputs. The preservative generally used in bottling wine is sulfur dioxide, also called sulfite. In Europe, a wine bottled without sulfite cannot be labelled 'organic' unless the grapes were grown organically. However not all organic wine is made without sulfur. At present, in most countries wine makers are not legally required to list added ingredients on the wine label.

Not all wine producers who use organic or biodynamic methods apply for certification. So, for anyone seriously interested in buying organic wine, a reliable wine guide is useful and a good wine merchant will also give advice on how to choose organic.

Quality grains

Organic spirits must be made from grains, fruits and herbs that are grown organically. Since organic grains cannot be preserved with chemical fungicides they must be stored in silos with very low humidity, and it is claimed that this treatment helps them to retain many micro-organisms that help provide a smooth and clean flavour. Organic herbs used in gin have more natural oils than inorganic, which give the drink a powerful, fresh and complex taste. Consumer response to organic spirits has been enthusiastic and they are increasingly widely available.

food

Modern thinking on healthy eating endorses the old adage that 'a little of what you fancy does you good' – make it organic and it will benefit you and the environment. The most important dietary advice is to eat a wide variety of foods, including several portions of fresh fruit and vegetables every day.

Even though we are all encouraged to reduce our consumption of saturated fats and sugar, what the food industry calls 'low-fat' or 'sugar-free' does not mean that these highly processed foods are nutritionally sound. It is always best to go for unprocessed oils and real butter rather than substitutes. The best oils are labelled 'organic' and 'cold-pressed' – cold pressing retains more of the oils' nutrients. Avoid vegetable oils that are promoted as being low in saturated fats as these are usually highly processed. Part of changing to an organic lifestyle is likely to mean a change in eating habits where you eat smaller quantities of the things that do you good rather than larger amounts of processed food.

For anyone not on an exclusively plant-based diet, organically produced meat, poultry and dairy products are a perfect choice. Organic meat is reared naturally with high regard for animal welfare, and fed an organic diet. The result is firm and delicious meat with a good amount of fat, and once you have cooked and eaten organic you'll never want to return to intensively reared meat.

cooking
organic

Cooking organic means choosing the best food and preparing it with care before cooking it to preserve the maximum goodness, presenting it with thought and storing it carefully. Care taken in the selection and preparation of food never goes unrewarded.

Cooking methods

Fish and lean cuts of meat have little fat to lubricate them so cook them quickly to avoid them drying out and becoming tough. Grilling or flash-frying in a little oil or butter is quick and easy. Add extra fat to even substantial cuts of meat and poultry when they are roasted in the oven to keep them moist, and leaner cuts of meat in stews should be given an extra helping of fat by browning them first. Fat is also an excellent carrier of flavour.

Green vegetables lose colour, flavour and nutrients by overcooking but this loss can be kept to a minimum by cooking them rapidly in enough boiling water just to cover them, or steaming them so that they are still green with a slight bite. Root vegetables, and also pumpkins and the other squashes, retain more nutrients if they are cooked without water by baking them in the oven. Aubergines taste wonderful when they are baked, cut-side down with just a film of oil to keep them from sticking.

Grating vegetables such as carrots and courgettes allows them to be very rapidly sautéed – cooked through but still crunchy and full of goodness. Thinly sliced potatoes cook in a short time and can also be steamed. Don't soak them first as this leaches out much of their vitamin content. Stew fruit in just enough water to keep it from sticking and don't discard the liquid.

Fresh versus frozen

Almost all food tastes better when it is fresh and crisp but it is handy to have frozen food to hand. Freshly picked vegetables, bread and some cooked dishes freeze well and many cooks prepare an extra serving of main dishes and even puddings to freeze when they are cooking. Thaw frozen food thoroughly before cooking and never refreeze it. When you buy frozen food get it home and into your freezer as soon as possible and if it has thawed on the way home prepare it straight away.

Safe cold storage

A well-stocked refrigerator does not mean one that is stuffed to the gills with so much food that there isn't an inch of space for one more item. To keep the temperature safe (0–5°C/32–41°F), it is vital that there is room for air to circulate. In a refrigerator with a freezing compartment the coldest shelves are those just below it. In a refrigerator the coldest shelves are at the bottom. Keep fish and meat in the coldest area of your refrigerator, and always keep raw meat and fish separate from cooked, and away from dairy products.

Cheese and other dairy products, opened cartons and jars can go on the upper shelves or in the refrigerator door. Keep salad vegetables unwrapped and unwashed in the salad drawer with plenty of space for air to circulate, which will keep items crisper longer. Make sure everything is covered, especially items such as butter, cream and milk, which can absorb flavours from other foods. Always allow hot food to cool completely before putting it into the refrigerator.

Avoid risks

Food that is very cold or very hot is much less vulnerable to bacterial contamination than food that is lukewarm as bacteria thrive in the temperatures in between. If you are reheating leftovers make sure they are heated right through and it is not really a good idea to reheat them more than once. Throw away anything that smells even slightly 'off' and never scrape off mould. Not all moulds are toxic but some are deadly. The mould that is visible is the fruiting body of the organism and even though you can't see them ungerminated spores may have invaded the rest of the item. Even if your granny always scraped the mould off the top of the jam pot and was never sick a day in her life, don't do this yourself!

Cooking utensils

Try and limit the use of plastic items in your kitchen by opting for wood and recycled glass instead whenever possible. It is hard to avoid using metal cooking utensils but be aware that small amounts of some metals can be transferred to the food itself. Aluminium in particular is to be avoided in cooking as it can leach from saucepans and kitchen foil into acidic foods to form aluminium salts. Results of research into the role of aluminium in health problems are inconclusive, but if you do have any old bare aluminium pans you should replace them with stainless steel ones. Similarly, use kitchen foil sparingly, replacing it with greaseproof paper whenever possible.

fruit and vegetables

The ideal healthy diet is built on an exciting variety of fresh fruits and vegetables. For optimum benefit, servings of raw vegetables and fruit juice should be on the daily menu. Crudités or crunchy salads are a good way of incorporating fresh raw foods into your diet. Or invest in a juicer and experiment with various combinations.

Naturally fresh and ripe

The best place to buy fresh produce is at a local organic shop or farm you trust. Here you know the food will be fresh, brimming with goodness and with no unwanted additives. If there is no farm shop near you, supermarkets do sell a good range of organic produce but look carefully at the label for place of origin and sell-by date.

Organic fruit is not only chemical-free, it is more nutritious and has a fuller flavour because it is likely to have been allowed to ripen naturally on the bush or tree. This means that fruits are usually richest in valuable vitamins, they also taste sweeter because the riper the fruit, the greater the sugar content. The flavour is fuller and more complex than fruit that is picked green and kept in storage.

The skin of organically grown fruit and vegetables has not been treated with preservatives so you have only to wash items rather than peel them, and the skin or peel is often a good source of fibre and nutrients.

Storage solutions

Heat, damp and light are the enemies of freshness. It is always best to eat produce when it is as fresh as possible or store it in a cool dark, dry place such as an airy larder. However, few houses now have such a space so there are other ways of keeping produce as fresh as possible for as long as possible.

Most leafy vegetables can be kept in the refrigerator for two or three days until you are ready to use them. Salad greens, spring onions, chillies, peppers, leeks and root ginger all keep reasonably well in the salad drawer of a refrigerator but have a better flavour at room temperature. Celery and parsley can be stored in a jug of water, as long as you change the water daily. Do not put tomatoes in the refrigerator – not only do they lose their own flavour but they can absorb flavours from elsewhere. Slightly under-ripe tomatoes can be stored in a dark drawer where they will ripen while keeping maximum flavour. There is no advantage in keeping citrus fruit in the refrigerator, although you can freeze oranges for making jam.

Do not refrigerate tropical treats such as bananas, pine-apples or avocados. Try and purchase them ripe for eating but if they are not ripe when you buy them they will soften eventually if you simply keep them in the fruit bowl. Use avocados as soon as they begin to be soft to the touch, before the skin starts to darken, and try not to bruise them as the green flesh will turn black wherever there is a dent.

Squash, pumpkins, potatoes and root vegetables should be stored in a cool, dark and dry place – covering them with a basket or paper bag on a cool floor is fine if storage space is limited. Onions should be stored in fresh, cool air. Hang them in a net bag or an old stocking rather than leaving them in a basket or bowl. If you use only half an onion in a recipe, put the other half in greaseproof paper or in a covered dish in the refrigerator. Never wrap it in aluminium foil or clingfilm, and always keep it away from dairy products.

Canned vegetables

Many brands of organic canned vegetables are packed in lined tins. This ensures that there will be no trace of aluminium in them. Organic canned tomatoes and beans are very useful staples; chickpeas are very versatile store cupboard items, too, useful for houmous and as a nutritious instant addition to soups, salads, stews and casseroles. Canned tomatoes are often better than out-of-season fresh tomatoes and many brands do not have any added sugar. If they have added flavourings such as basil this, too, will have been organically grown.

Fresh from the freezer

Many green vegetables, particularly peas and beans of all types, stand up well to freezing and, unlike most other frozen foods, can be cooked without thawing. Packets of peeled and sliced organic vegetables are useful standbys for emergency meal preparation. Fresh vegetables generally have a much better texture than frozen, but vegetables frozen immediately after picking do have more nutritional value than vegetables that have been hanging around the kitchen for a while, so it is always useful to have a packet or two in the freezer.

Canned and dried fruit

Organic fruit canned in natural juice is now widely available, and can be useful for some occasions, but it is usually easy to find such a wide variety of fresh organic fruit that there is little need for canned. If you do buy canned fruit, check the labelling carefully and avoid fruit packed with added sugar as this can detract from its taste and texture.

Dried fruit, on the other hand, is definitely a necessary staple in any store cupboard. While non-organic dried fruit is often coated with oil, which may be made from genetically modified material, you can be sure that organic dried fruit is uncoated; nor is it treated with sulfur to preserve the colour.

Traditionally, dried fruits were valuable sources of vitamins during the winter months when fresh fruit was not so widely available. The sweets we still delight in at Christmas, the time of the winter solstice, are an evocative reminder of how important dried fruit and spices once were in previous centuries. When fruit is dried the sugar it contains becomes very concentrated, and a handful of dried apricots, cranberries, cherries, figs, raisins or a few slices of dried apple, banana, papaya or pear are a wonderful source of quick energy. Dried fruit may be high in sugar but it is also packed full of essential micro-nutrients such as zinc and potassium; dried figs are a good way of getting extra calcium.

Dried pulses

Dried pulses are among the most useful foods to have in the store cupboard. They should be stored in air-tight containers away from strong light. Always soak dried beans for a time before cooking, but never longer than overnight as they may ferment. It is a good idea to cover them with boiling water, leave them for ten or fifteen minutes, pour off the water and then leave them to soak in fresh cold water for a few hours. Lentils do not need to be soaked before cooking.

Historic flavours

Hand in hand with the move towards the increasing popularity of organic produce is the revival of interest in old varieties of both fruit and vegetables. Organic farmers have a vested interest in biodiversity and are much more likely to plant a wider variety of fruit and vegetables than the farmer who relies on a monocrop. Thus organic growers are often responsible for the preservation of ancient species. Because they are less reliant on agri-chemicals they need to find varieties suited to their own individual growing conditions. Interest in diversity also preserves old traditions such as perry-making, which had almost died out in Britain until the rise of organics and the renewed interest in good local produce and history.

The multiples are naturally jumping on the varietal bandwagon and the larger stores are attempting to reintroduce a few of the old favourites – you can now buy 'heirloom' potatoes and tomatoes, as well as a wide variety of brassicas and local apples and pears. Farmers' markets, too, are always a good source of more old-fashioned varieties of fruit and vegetables, as well as more unusual crops. A small producer who sells locally is able to grow a much wider variety of produce than someone growing for the national or international market because he is not reliant on the big stores' criteria of long-keeping qualities and uniformity. They are also likely to be able to tell you something about the background of the produce, and the best way to cook it.

Residual dangers

Buy organic to keep safe: a recent UK survey revealed that two-thirds of all of the fruit and vegetables on sale in several big-name stores contained chemical residues.

- Fruit and vegetables that are grown conventionally are routinely treated with fungicides, pesticides and insecticides as well as growth regulators
- Up to 70 per cent of fruit and vegetables contain residues of pesticides
- Pesticide residues in non-organically grown produce are higher than ever before
- Chemicals actually enter into the growing plants and cannot be removed simply by washing and peeling
- The skin of non-organic fruit may be coated with preservative-containing wax
- Conventionally grown apples and pears are treated with potentially dangerous chemicals including the organophosphate chlorpyrifos and the controversial pesticide chlormequat
- Even where residues in produce are below the legal limit, scientists now suspect a potential danger through constant and accumulative exposure to agricultural chemicals
- A combination of residues from chemical applications may be more toxic than any single element on its own
- Since public health regulations are less stringent in certain countries, you can never be quite sure what pesticides you are buying when you buy imported inorganic food

vegetable recipes

Hot Spicy Gazpacho

Although conventionally served chilled, this vibrant soup is served warm here with a sprinkling of crunchy croûtons.

Preparation time: 20 minutes • Cooking time: 15 minutes • 300 calories per serving • Serves 4 as a starter

What you need

900g (2lb) very ripe cherry tomatoes • 1 cucumber, peeled, halved lengthways and deseeded • 1 garlic clove, chopped • 1 red chilli, deseeded and finely chopped • 2 spring onions, finely chopped • 60ml (4 tbsp) extra-virgin olive oil • 15ml (1 tbsp) red wine vinegar • 1 tbsp golden caster sugar • salt and freshly ground black pepper • paprika and fresh wild rocket, to garnish
For the croûtons: 75g (3oz) ciabatta, cut into small cubes • 60ml (4 tbsp) extra-virgin olive oil • large pinch each of sea salt flakes and paprika

What to do

1. To make the croûtons, preheat the oven to 190°C/375°F/Gas Mark 5. Place the bread in a bowl, add the oil and sprinkle with sea salt flakes and paprika. Toss everything together and transfer the croûtons to a baking tray. Cook for 10 minutes, until golden brown, turning occasionally.
2. To make the soup, process all the ingredients, except the seasoning and garnishes, in a food processor or blender until smooth. Transfer the soup to a saucepan and heat gently until warm, then season to taste.
3. To serve, spoon the warm soup into mugs or bowls, top each one with a few croûtons, sprinkle over a little paprika and garnish with a rocket leaf.

Rocket and Onion Salad

Organic wild rocket has a distinctive peppery taste, which is complemented by the sweetness of the white onion and lemony dressing.

Preparation time: 10 minutes • 55 calories per serving • Serves: 4

What you need

1 small white onion, finely sliced • 225g (8oz) rocket • grated lemon rind, to garnish • **For the dressing:** salt and freshly ground black pepper • 30ml (2 tbsp) lemon juice • 60ml (4 tbsp) olive oil

What to do

1. To make the dressing, place the seasoning in a small bowl and whisk in the lemon juice and olive oil.
2. To make the salad, place the onion in a large bowl with the rocket. Pour the dressing over the salad, toss well, then garnish with grated lemon rind. Serve either in a large salad bowl or on individual plates.

Chestnut Mushroom Gratin

This warming main course is made with readily available organic ingredients. Serve it with steamed vegetables or a green salad.

Preparation time: 15 minutes • Cooking time: 35 minutes • 410 calories per serving • Serves 4

What you need

700g (1½lb) small sweet potatoes, peeled and halved • 50g (2oz) butter • 700g (1½lb) chestnut mushrooms, quartered • 150ml (¼ pint) dry white wine • 100ml (3½fl oz) crème fraîche • 1 tsp chopped fresh thyme • salt and freshly ground black pepper • 3 tbsp fresh white breadcrumbs • 5 tbsp freshly grated Parmesan cheese

What to do

1. Cook the sweet potatoes in boiling salted water until just tender, then drain and allow to cool. Cut the potatoes into 5mm (¼in) slices and set aside.

2. Melt half the butter in a large frying pan until it starts to foam. Add half the mushrooms and fry over a high heat for 2–3 minutes, remove from the pan and set aside. Repeat with the remaining butter and mushrooms.

3. Add the wine to the pan, bring to the boil and allow to bubble until reduced by half. Add the crème fraîche and leave to bubble for a further 2–3 minutes. Return the mushrooms to the pan with the thyme and seasoning.

4. Preheat the oven to 190°C/375°F/Gas Mark 5. Turn the mushrooms into a 1.4 litre (2½ pint) ovenproof dish and arrange the potato slices around the edge in an overlapping layer. Mix together the breadcrumbs and Parmesan and sprinkle over the potatoes. Cook for 15 minutes, or until heated through and golden.

Chestnut Mushroom Gratin

fruit recipes

Apple and Blackberry Snow

Blackberries are a natural partner to apples. Try picking them in the wild to add to the fun!

Preparation time: 15 minutes, plus 1 hour chilling • Cooking time: 12 minutes • 125 calories per serving • Serves 6

What you need

900g (2lb) cooking apples, peeled and sliced • 60ml (4 tbsp) fruit juice • grated rind of 1 lemon • 225g (8oz) blackberries • 6 tbsp caster sugar • 1 large egg white • mint sprigs, to decorate

What to do

1. Place the sliced apples and fruit juice in a saucepan and cook, uncovered, over a low heat for 10 minutes, or until soft. Transfer the apples to a food processor and blend until smooth. Stir in the lemon rind, cover, and leave to chill for 1 hour.
2. Place the blackberries and half of the caster sugar in a saucepan and heat gently for 2–3 minutes, or until the blackberries begin to soften and the juices run.
3. Whisk the egg white until stiff, adding the remaining caster sugar gradually until the mixture forms stiff peaks. Fold the stiff egg white into the apple purée.
4. Divide the blackberries and their juice between six serving glasses. Spoon the apple mixture on top of the blackberries, decorate with mint sprigs and serve.

Note: The young, the elderly, pregnant women and those suffering from immune deficiency diseases should not eat raw or lightly cooked eggs.

Apricots with Caramelized Nuts

This dessert can be made in advance and frozen for up to three months. Follow the recipe up to step 2, then allow to cool before freezing.

Preparation time: 20 minutes • Cooking time: 45 minutes • 455 calories per serving for 4 ; 300 calories per serving for 6 • Serves 4–6

What you need

700g (1½lb) firm apricots • 50g (2oz) butter • 125g (4oz) caster sugar • 100ml (3½fl oz) orange juice • vanilla ice cream, to serve • **For the caramelized nuts:** 75g (3oz) whole skinned almonds • 125g (4oz) caster sugar

What to do

1. Preheat the oven to 200°C/400°F/Gas Mark 6. Slice the apricots along one side (so they still remain whole) and remove the stones. Put the apricots in an ovenproof dish.
2. Gently melt the butter and sugar in a saucepan, stirring occasionally, until golden, then remove from the heat. Carefully stir in the orange juice (it may splutter as the sugar hardens into lumps). Return the mixture to a low heat and stir until the sugar has dissolved. Pour the liquid over the apricots.
3. Bake the apricots for 45 minutes, or until just soft, spooning the liquid over the fruit from time to time. Set aside and allow to cool. (Remove the apricot skins at this stage if you like.)
4. Meanwhile, caramelize the nuts. Put the almonds in a pan of cold water, bring to the boil and simmer for 2 minutes. Drain and cut the nuts into thick shreds. (They will be soft enough to chop without splintering.) Place the pieces under a hot grill and toast until golden.

5. Put the sugar and 150ml (¼ pint) water in a pan. Bring to the boil and allow to bubble until the syrup turns a deep golden caramel. Take the pan off the heat and stir in 50ml (4 tbsp) warm water. Return the pan to the heat and stir in the almonds. Serve the apricots with scoops of vanilla ice cream and spoon the caramelized nuts on top.

Passion fruit, Banana and Grape Smoothie

Smoothies make a nutritious and filling start to the day. Live, mild-tasting bio yogurt contains beneficial bacteria, which are good for the digestive system.

Preparation time: 5 minutes, plus 30 minutes chilling • 120 calories per serving • Serves 4

What you need

4 ripe passion fruit • 150ml (¼ pint) low-fat bio yogurt, plus 15ml (1 tbsp) to decorate • 8 ice cubes, crushed • 4 ripe bananas, about 550g (1¼lb) total weight, roughly chopped • 225g (8oz) seedless white grapes

What to do

1. Chill four tall glasses in the freezer. Cut the passion fruit in half and remove the pulp. Reserve 15ml (1 tbsp) of the pulp, place the rest in a blender with the remaining ingredients and process until smooth. (The passion fruit pips will remain whole.)

2. Serve the smoothie in the chilled glasses, decorated with 15ml (1 tbsp) of yogurt mixed with the reserved passion fruit pulp.

Apricots with Caramelized Nuts

organic
eggs

Eggs bearing the organic label are free of any genetically modified organisms. They contain no potentially dangerous residues of antibiotics, hormones or the artificial colouring that makes yolks unnaturally bright yellow. And, not only are organic eggs better for our health than the cheap ones produced by intensive battery hen farming, organic principles mean a better quality of life for the hens laying the eggs.

Organic certification

All organic eggs are free-range but not all free-range eggs have been produced to organic standards. If you are not largely restricted to urban and supermarket shopping you can often also find unaccredited organic eggs from small producers up and down the country.

For maximum safety it is advisable that all eggs, even organic ones, that are going to be eaten by infants, pregnant women and anyone who is elderly or ill should be cooked thoroughly until the yolk is solid. Foods containing raw eggs such as mayonnaise or royal icing are best avoided completely.

Interest in health, taste and diversity has led to a renewed interest in some of the old breeds of hen just as much as it has with old varieties of fruit and vegetables. At the top end of the egg market are those eggs that come from named, rare-breed birds kept in small flocks. When there is no mention of organic certification it is up to the consumer to decide whether or not these eggs are worth the extra expense. If you are seriously concerned that they are not certified organic, ask the producer why not – it may simply be that their flock is too small to warrant the expense of annual accreditation.

Buying safe

Free-range organic eggs are the only eggs that can be virtually guaranteed completely safe from the possibilities, however slim, of infections. At the other end of the market are hens' eggs from intensive rearing systems. Battery farming and egg production led to one of the most widely reported food scares in recent years – salmonella in eggs. Although this disease is seldom fatal in humans, it causes violent food poisoning, vomiting and acute stomach distress, which can last for several days and can be more serious for anyone who is already unwell or with a compromised immune system.

The infection can be spread by contaminated chicken feed, or it can be circulated and transmitted by air. Chickens housed in badly ventilated sheds where there is a high concentration of ammonia, which irritates the respiratory tract, are particularly at risk. The infection affects hens' lungs, liver, spleen, kidneys, ovary and oviduct, and diseased birds then excrete the bacteria for almost a month so that cross-contamination is extremely high. It can be eliminated by practising good animal husbandry, as proved in Sweden, where a campaign to clean up the poultry industry has resulted in the virtual eradication of salmonella.

Battery conditions

We should all think twice before buying cheap eggs. In addition to the threat of salmonella infection in battery chicken houses, hens spend their short lives in appalling conditions in these rearing sheds. Fortunately, pressure for purer food and government legislation is helping to change the situation, but currently four hens can still be confined together in a claustrophobic wire cage the size of an A4 sheet of paper. A hen's claws may become twisted around the mesh and her bones brittle from lack of exercise; close proximity to her cage mates causes aggression so hens are often painfully debeaked. The lights are left on to encourage maximum laying and, when egg production drops off at about seventy-two weeks, the redundant hens are jammed into unhygienic containers with no food and water and sent off to slaughter. Their meat is then used for processed food at the lower end of the food chain – in pies, pet food, soups and stock cubes.

Free-range organic eggs criteria

Free-range organic eggs in the UK are strictly regulated for Soil Association accreditation.

- Chicken flocks cannot number more than 500 birds
- Their antibiotic-free diet must be at least 70 per cent organic
- Their diet must not contain any animal protein or colorants
- Chickens are not debeaked
- Organic poultry and egg producers are regularly inspected

milk, cream and yogurt

Milk from cows, goats, sheep and buffaloes has been made into foods, which have been invaluable staples of the European diet for millennia. Milk is a wonderful source of bone-building calcium and other essential nutrients.

Growing dairy market

Dairy products are now the fastest-growing sector among organic foods. Indeed, an organic yogurt has become the leading brand in the UK, even outselling own-label versions of natural yogurt, which is very encouraging to everyone involved in producing and promoting organic foods. It proves beyond doubt that if a particular organic product is available at a competitive price and if it delivers on quality and taste, customers will respond with enthusiasm.

Types of milk

Organic dairy products are now widely available, but which ones should you choose? It is not necessary, and may even be dangerous, for growing children to eat low-fat foods – unless of course they become dangerously overweight. Fat is a major source of vitamins D and E. However, for anyone who does carry more body fat than is healthy or aesthetically acceptable, reducing the dietary intake of saturated fat is a very wise move. In this case, low-fat, skimmed and semi-skimmed milk products can be helpful in your diet.

It is not easy to purchase unpasteurized milk, which is raw milk straight from the farm. It contains high levels of micro-organisms that have been considered potentially dangerous to some groups of consumer – particularly the very young, the very old and the sick. But if there is a supplier near you, it is worth trying as unpasteurized milk tastes quite different from pasteurized. Pasteurization involves heating the milk to almost boiling point for a few seconds and then cooling it. After this process most milk is then homogenized, which distributes the fat particles through the liquid. Some milks marketed as 'breakfast milk' or 'extra-creamy' have additional fat particles added to them at this stage.

UHT, or ultra heat-treated (long-life), milk is heated to 138°C/280°F in the container in which it will be sold, which enables it to be stored at room temperature for up to three months. Once opened, however, it should be kept in the refrigerator. Buttermilk is what is left when milk is churned and all the fat extracted to be made into butter. Most commercial buttermilk is made by adding a bacteria culture to low-fat or skimmed milk. It is often used in baking as the acid it contains reacts with baking soda to release a gas, which acts as a rising agent. It is very refreshing to drink. Fat-reduced milks – skimmed and semi-skimmed – are a valuable source of calcium without the fat, but be sure to replace the protein in your diet. Check the nutritional information on the label of low-fat and fat-free dairy products, and consider whether it might be better simply to have smaller quantities of a full-fat, unadulterated product.

Creams and yogurts

Organic creams range from full-fat to smooth, less fatty alternatives such as fromage frais and crème fraîche. Both of these have an agreeable, slightly sour flavour and are a useful substitute for thick cream for anyone watching their weight. Yogurts also range from full to zero fat. If you opt for a zero-fat yogurt check the label to see there are no thickeners added for bulk; proper natural yogurt is made from milk and the particular bacteria or culture that turns it into yogurt and nothing else. 'Live' or bio yogurts are said to contain more of the live bacteria that is good for the gut but there is some debate as to whether or not the bacteria actually survive processing in quantities enough to make a difference.

cheese

Cheese, milk and other milk products – cream, butter, yogurt and so on – are among the most nutrient-dense and valuable additions to a varied, balanced diet. Such dairy products constitute a very important food group on which to concentrate when choosing organic.

Wide selection

In France, it is said that there is a different cheese for every day of the year. Certainly, there are many different varieties and any specialist cheese merchant and some of the larger supermarkets will have an outstanding selection of superb organic cheeses of every type – from traditional cow's milk cheeses to those from sheep and goats. Organic cheese must be made from organic milk and any additional flavourings such as herbs or garlic must also be grown to organic standards. Organic cheese can be made with animal or vegetable rennet, but vegetarian cheese is never made with animal rennet, a substance that occurs naturally in the stomachs of ruminant animals and is a traditional cheese-making ingredient.

Dairy products are vitally important nutritionally for ovo-lacto vegetarians, but be careful with the kind of vegetarian cheese you purchase. If it is not organic it may be made with bacterial rennets or an enzyme called chymosin which was created by adding genetic material from calf cells to yeast. Chymosin is now approved by the Vegetarian Society but is never used in organic vegetarian cheese, which is made only with rennet of fungal or bacterial origin.

Organic dairy farming

Organic dairy farming does not routinely employ antibiotics in feed, as medicine, or to promote growth; furthermore, it respects the welfare of the cows.

- In organic herds fewer cows go lame and suffer from udder infections such as mastitis
- Mastitis now occurs in roughly 35 per cent of cows per annum in a conventional herd and is treated with massive doses of antibiotics. Milk from an infected cow that is not exhibiting symptoms can contain the bacteria even when the milk is tested, since testing for this infection is not part of the milk-monitoring process; humans can suffer from vomiting and diarrhoea and food and blood poisoning from ingesting mastitis-infected milk
- Organic farmers do not routinely dose their healthy animals with antibiotics and medicines
- Organic milk contains no growth hormones or other additives
- Organic dairy farmers in general have high standards of animal welfare, allowing calves access to their mothers for much longer than the two or three days allowed in conventional herds, and providing cows indoors with the space to lie down comfortably in barns

Unpasteurized cheeses

There is considerable controversy about cheeses made from unpasteurized (raw) milk. Cheese-makers insist that the cheese-making process destroys any potentially dangerous organisms and that some beneficial organisms in unpasteurized milk and cream are killed off in the heating process of pasteurization. They do have the science to prove it. The flavour may also suffer in pasteurization and contamination is much more likely to occur during transport or storage or if the pasteurizing process is faulty. Some of the most famous French cheeses, Roquefort among them, are legally required to be made only with raw milk. In the US, there is a move to ban the sale of unpasteurized cheese, which has caused an uproar among specialist cheese-sellers and gourmets alike.

Soft cheeses

Delicious, organic soft cheeses are available, often made by small producers from goat's and ewe's milk, as well as cow's. Or you can make your own very easily by letting organic milk turn, then leaving it to strain and adding herbs and seasonings of your choice. In the late 1980s, soft cheese became a high-risk food when two dozen babies in the UK died from listeriosis within a three-year period. The UK government officially warned pregnant women, the ill and elderly to avoid all soft cheeses – not specifically those made from raw milk. Be careful how you handle all food products; store dairy products in a refrigerator rather than at room temperature or above, and always buy organic to lessen the risk of food allergies or adverse reactions.

cheese and egg recipes

Cheese and Chive Tart

This delicately textured, creamy tart can be prepared in advance and frozen.

Preparation time: 10 minutes (20 minutes if making pastry by hand), plus 35 minutes chilling • Cooking time: 55 minutes • 516 calories per serving for 6; 387 calories per serving for 8 • Serves 6–8

What you need

200g (7oz) plain flour • 100g (3½oz) chilled butter, diced • salt, freshly ground black pepper and cayenne pepper • 25g (1oz) Parmesan or Cheddar cheese, grated • 4 large eggs • 125g (4oz) creamy goat's cheese • 100ml (3½fl oz) crème fraîche • 2 tbsp chopped fresh chives • ground nutmeg, to taste • 250g (9oz) goat's cheese with rind

What to do

1. Put the flour in a food processor with the butter and a pinch each of salt and cayenne pepper. Whizz until the mixture resembles breadcrumbs. Add the grated cheese and one egg, then whizz or stir together until combined – you might need to add a little cold water. (To make the pastry by hand, rub the flour and butter together until the mixture resembles breadcrumbs, add the cheese and one egg, stir to combine.) Turn out the dough, wrap in greaseproof paper and chill for 20 minutes.
2. Preheat the oven to 200°C/400°F/Gas Mark 6. Roll out the pastry on a lightly floured surface into a circle large enough to line a 23cm (9in) x 2.5cm (1in) deep loose-bottomed tart tin. Press the pastry into the tin, prick the base with a fork and line with greaseproof paper and baking beans. Bake for 15 minutes, then remove the paper and beans and return to the oven for 5–10 minutes, until cooked to the centre.
3. Lightly whisk one egg and brush over the inside of the pastry case. Reduce the oven to 180°C/350°F/Gas Mark 4 and return the pastry case to the oven for 1 minute.
4. Mix the remaining two eggs with the creamy goat's cheese, crème fraîche and chives; season with pepper and a pinch of ground nutmeg. Crumble the rinded cheese into the egg mixture and pour the filling into the pastry case. Bake for 25–30 minutes, or until just set.
5. Allow to cool for 15 minutes, then remove from the tin. Serve warm with new potatoes and salad or vegetables.

Goat's Cheese and Walnut Salad

This is a perfect salad for a light lunch, served with chunks of crusty bread.

Preparation time: 5 minutes • 390 calories per serving • Serves 6

What you need

30ml (2 tbsp) red wine vinegar • 125ml (4fl oz) olive oil • large pinch of caster sugar • salt and freshly ground black pepper • 1 large radicchio, shredded • 2 bunches of prepared watercress, about 125g (4oz) total weight • 1 red onion, finely sliced • 150g (5oz) walnut pieces • 2 x 100g (3½oz) packets goat's cheese, crumbled

What to do

1. To make the salad dressing, mix together the red wine vinegar, olive oil, caster sugar and seasoning in a bowl. Put to one side.

2. Put the radicchio, watercress and onion in a large bowl. Pour the dressing over the salad and toss well.

3. Sprinkle with the walnuts and goat's cheese and serve.

Dolcelatte and Prune Crostini

Dried fruit is an unusual but healthy and delicious addition to this crostini.

Preparation time: 10 minutes • Cooking time: 5 minutes • 425 calories per serving • Serves 4

What you need

175g (6oz) Dolcelatte or Gorgonzola cheese, crumbled • 75g (3oz) pitted ready-to-eat prunes or dates, roughly chopped • 50g (2oz) walnuts, chopped • 1 tsp chopped fresh rosemary • freshly ground black pepper • 4–8 slices of ciabatta • olive oil, to drizzle • rosemary sprigs and coarse sea salt, to garnish

What to do

1. Mix the crumbled Dolcelatte or Gorgonzola with the prunes or dates, walnuts, rosemary and freshly ground black pepper.

2. Lightly toast the ciabatta, drizzle with olive oil and spoon the cheese and prune mixture on top. Place under a hot grill until the cheese has melted. Garnish with rosemary sprigs and sea salt, then serve.

Dolcelatte and Prune Crostini

Spinach and Feta Frittata

Spinach and Feta Frittata

These individual-sized frittatas are accompanied by a refreshing tomato dressing.

Preparation time: 20 minutes • Cooking time: 12 minutes • 260 calories per serving • Serves 4

What you need

200g (7oz) baby leeks, cut into 2.5cm (1in) pieces • 6 large eggs • 60ml (4 tbsp) semi-skimmed milk • freshly grated nutmeg, to taste • 125g (4oz) feta cheese, diced • 125g (4oz) fresh young spinach leaves • 15ml (1 tbsp) olive oil • basil sprigs, to garnish • **For the dressing:** 15ml (1 tbsp) lemon juice • 30ml (2 tbsp) olive oil • 3 tbsp chopped spring onion tops • salt and freshly ground black pepper • 3 ripe tomatoes, skinned, deseeded and chopped

What to do

1. To make the dressing, whisk together the lemon juice, olive oil, spring onion tops and seasoning. Add the tomatoes and set aside.

2. Blanch the leeks until softened, then drain. Refresh the leeks in cold water, drain again and dry on kitchen paper.

3. Whisk the eggs, milk, a little seasoning and nutmeg together. Stir in the feta, leeks and spinach.

4. Heat the oil in a non-stick frying pan. Place four 10cm (4in) poaching rings in the pan and pour a quarter of the egg mixture into each one. Fry gently for 4–5 minutes, until just set.

5. Place the frittatas under a hot grill and cook until the tops are golden and they are just firm to the touch. Turn the frittatas out of their poaching rings, garnish with basil sprigs and serve with the tomato dressing.

Piperade

Scrambled eggs with a twist, this classic French recipe can be served with a green salad and country-style bread.

Preparation time: 10 minutes • Cooking time: 25 minutes • 309 calories per serving • Serves 4

What you need

30ml (2 tbsp) olive oil • 1 onion, finely chopped • 1 garlic clove, finely chopped • 1 red pepper, deseeded and chopped • 375g (13oz) tomatoes, skinned, deseeded and chopped • pinch of cayenne pepper • salt and freshly ground black pepper • 8 large eggs, lightly whisked • chopped fresh flat-leaf parsley, to garnish

What to do

1. Heat the oil in a heavy-based frying pan, add the onion and garlic and cook gently for 5 minutes. Add the red pepper and cook for 10 minutes, or until softened.
2. Add the tomatoes, increase the heat and cook until they have reduced to a thick pulp. Season well with cayenne pepper, salt and freshly ground black pepper.
3. Add the eggs to the frying pan. Using a wooden spoon, stir gently until they just begin to set but are still creamy. Garnish with parsley and serve immediately.

Poached Eggs and Ham with Chive Butter Sauce

A perfect Sunday brunch or light supper dish, which needs little in the way of accompaniments.

Preparation time: 10 minutes • Cooking time: 30 minutes • 840 calories per serving • Serves 4

What you need

30ml (2 tbsp) white wine vinegar • 4 large eggs • 200g (7oz) cooked ham, sliced • 4 muffins, halved and toasted • baby spinach leaves and fresh chives, to garnish • **For the chive butter sauce:** 30ml (2 tbsp) white wine vinegar • 2 large egg yolks • 250g (9oz) unsalted butter • 15ml (1 tbsp) lemon juice • salt and freshly ground black pepper • 3 tbsp chopped fresh chives

What to do

1. To make the sauce, place the white wine vinegar and 15ml (1 tbsp) water in a small saucepan. Bring to the boil and allow to bubble until reduced by half.
2. Place the egg yolks in a blender or food processor and whizz for 1–2 minutes, then pour in the reduced vinegar. Melt the butter in a small pan then, with the blender on full speed, immediately pour the butter in a thin, steady stream on to the egg yolk mixture. Add the lemon juice, season to taste, then stir in the chives. Set aside.
3. To poach the eggs, add the vinegar to a large pan of boiling water. Break an egg into a cup or ramekin. Swirl the boiling water to create a 'whirlpool' effect, then carefully tip the egg into the water. Cook very gently for 3–4 minutes, until the white is just set and the yolk still soft. Lift the egg out with a slotted spoon and place in a shallow dish of warm water. Repeat with the remaining eggs.
4. Divide the ham between the toasted muffins. Drain the eggs on kitchen paper and place on top of the ham. Spoon the butter sauce over the top. Place under a preheated grill and cook for 1–2 minutes, or until the top is golden. Garnish with baby spinach leaves, chives and freshly ground black pepper and serve immediately.

organic meat
and fish

Organically raised animals live healthier, longer lives, eat better food and, ultimately, are killed as humanely as possible. Organic meat is not cheap to produce and therefore costs the consumer a little more, but it is wholesome, safe and far superior in flavour and texture.

Traceability

Only meat, poultry and fish that carries the logo of one of the officially recognized certifying bodies is truly organic. The terms 'real meat', 'Scotch beef', 'free-range' and 'additive-free' are no indication that they have been produced to the strict, legally enforced organic standards that ensure traceability from birth to plate.

To qualify as organic all livestock must be born and bred on an organic farm. Farmers are liable for inspection at every stage of an animal's life – from birth to slaughter, from farm to abattoir to packer, processor and retailer. Many organic farms sell on-site, at farmers' markets or on the Internet; and eliminating the middle man means better value and more choice for the consumer. A visit to an organic farm is an ideal way of demonstrating to anyone who thinks meat only comes in plastic packages how it gets there. The creatures that provide the food on our plates deserve our respect.

Rich, full lives

Grazing animals such as cattle and sheep are raised on pasture that has not been treated with artificial fertilizers or chemical sprays; the absence of agri-chemicals encourages beneficial insect and bird life, and crops and pasture are rotated to enrich the soil naturally. Any additional food the animals are fed must be free from antibiotics, growth promoters, hormones, GMOs and must not contain material from other animals.

Flocks and herds on organic farms tend to be smaller and live outside except in extreme weather. This results in flesh that is firm and full of flavour. Beef calves stay with their mothers on many organic farms and because they live longer, they mature slowly and naturally. After slaughter the meat is hung on the bone, which further improves texture and flavour. Organic beef usually contains more fat than other beef, which is bred specially to be lean. The fat improves the texture and the taste, and the best beef is slightly marbled with a thick layer of fat on the outside.

Ancient breeds

Organic farmers need breeds of animals that can withstand the climate out of doors. Many of the older types of beef, sheep and pigs are better suited for the natural life than the animals bred for intensive rearing. In some cases, because they tend to put on fat, which keeps them warm in winter, the older breeds have been crossed with other varieties to satisfy the demand for leaner meat. But many British farmers maintain that, for taste, traditional cattle breeds such as Welsh Black and Hereford, pigs like the Gloucester Old Spot, Oxford Sandy and Black, Tamworth and Saddlebacks, and Hebridean and Welsh Mountain sheep still make the best eating. If it were not for enthusiastic organic producers these valuable breeds would probably die out and we would all be the poorer for it.

Animal welfare

Because all organically raised animals are less intensively reared, organic farmers do not generally need to employ practices such as stressful overcrowding and the docking of pigs' tails, tooth cutting and nose rings. Most animals are kept outdoors as much as possible rather than in intensive rearing sheds. All organic pork, for example, comes from pigs that have access to fields as well as shelter. When you buy organic you are not just buying chemical-free, you are also buying into an ethos of respect for the animals and their lives.

Chickens kept in smaller flocks can determine their own natural pecking order. This means less pecking in general so that they do not have to endure having their beaks burned off. They have more space in their barns and free access to green grass and tasty insects during the day. Organic farm chickens are not killed at six weeks like those that are intensively reared but are slaughtered between nine and twelve weeks, which results in a richer, more mature flavour. Some organic producers even hang their chickens between plucking and dressing, which makes them even tastier and gives a superb texture. Similarly, organically reared ducks have access to water, while their intensively reared relatives do not.

Organic chickens and ducks are available all year round and organic geese and turkeys are marketed at Christmas time. In the country, real game is relatively inexpensive – except for rare birds such as grouse, partridge and capercaillie – and easy to buy. Pigeon and rabbit are considered farm pests, in season throughout the year. All game is low in fat and exceptional in flavour, although an older specimen may be a trifle tough. Their feed is not strictly organic as they may feed on chemically treated farm crops but they are a popular choice for thrifty carnivores and far tastier than anything intensively farmed.

Wider choice

As well as the familiar meats now available in most supermarkets and an increasing number of high-street butchers, there are many more exciting choices for the organic consumer. Goat, for example, is finely flavoured and low in fat. Venison is now organically farmed, as is wild boar, which is dark in colour and its flavour described as somewhere between beef and venison. Mutton, from a sheep older than eighteen months, was once considered a great delicacy, favoured above lamb, which is much blander because it is slaughtered younger. Mutton should be cooked slowly for a long time and has a far greater depth and complexity of flavour than lamb.

Few aware consumers want to buy veal, as veal calves are traditionally taken from their mothers on day two, reared in confined crates in dark houses and bucket fed. However, some organic dairy herds rear male veal calves for six months with their nursing mothers, drinking gallons of milk, which makes them expensive, but the naturally rosy pink delicately flavoured flesh is worth the price.

Fish

Organic fish are a good source of protein and are low in both fat and calories. In addition, they are an excellent source of essential fish oils and contain high levels of omega-3 oils, which help lower blood cholesterol, thereby reducing the risk of strokes and helping the body against heart disease.

Organic fish farming is relatively new, but very different from the environmentally polluting activity of traditional intensive fish farming where the fish are often flabby and anaemic in flavour as they have little room to swim and nothing to do but eat rich, processed diets. Overcrowding makes non-organic farmed fish liable to bacterial and insect infestation such as lice, and they are routinely treated with antibiotics, which end up in their flesh.

Organic fish benefit from a greater freedom of space and the emphasis is on natural growth, thus cutting the reliance on medicines. The fish are fed organic diets with no artificial colour or GMOs and produced from sustainable and/or organic sources. The organic ethos promotes sustainability, so organic fish farmers tend to enforce proactive environmental measures, such as planting reed beds for the maintenance and enhancement of water quality, which further adds to the health and welfare

BSE

The terrifying disease Bovine Spongiform Encephalopathy, BSE or Mad Cow Disease, and the horrendous human variant Creutzveldt-Jacob, CJD, has threatened the entire beef industry. The disease causes brain damage and death. BSE is not a problem on organic farms.

● BSE is believed to have originated from feeding cattle with food containing by-products from slaughterhouses, such as waste material from dead sheep

● Organic producers do not use concentrated feed that may contain material from other animals

● It is thought that BSE may also be connected to organophosphate use in agriculture

● Organic producers do not use organophosphates, which may be hazardous for both animals and handlers

of fish; in addition, humane handling and harvest are paramount to the organic regime. Trout produced to organic standards are not pink like most farmed trout, but have their natural pale flesh.

Some wild fish are also called organic, even if not strictly certified as such. Wild fish are lean and firm fleshed because they lead extremely active lives. They are more expensive than farmed fish but their texture and flavour is worth the price if you want a treat for a special occasion. For wild fish to be 'organic' they must come from unpolluted waters such as around the remote community of St Helena which is about 1,000 miles from both South America and southern Africa, on no major shipping lanes, and with little industry. The fish must be caught with minimal environmental impact, for example with rods and lines, so that fishermen take from the sea only what they need with no danger to other aquatic life. The fishing system must be sustainable – anything that is caught must be naturally replaced. All fish must be recorded and traced back to the fisherman who caught them.

meat recipes

Steak with Chips

Choose sirloin or rump steaks for grilling as they have more flavour than fillet.

Preparation time: 15 minutes, plus 30 minutes soaking • Cooking time: 20 minutes • 669 calories per serving • Serves 2

What you need

350g (12oz) large floury potatoes, such as Maris Piper, peeled and cut into chips • groundnut oil, for deep-frying • 2 x sirloin or rump steaks, about 175g (6oz) each • salt and freshly ground black pepper

What to do

1. Soak the chips in cold water for 30 minutes, then drain and dry well. Heat the groundnut oil in a chip pan or deep-fat fryer to 170°C/ 350°F or until a chip rises to the surface as soon as it is dropped in the pan. Quarter fill the frying basket and cook the chips for 5 minutes, or until they just begin to colour. Drain and set aside. Repeat with the remaining chips.

2. Season the steaks with plenty of black pepper and cook for 2 minutes on each side if you like them rare, 3 minutes each side for medium rare and 5 minutes for well done. (Gentle finger prodding is a good method of testing steak – if it feels soft like your cheek, it is rare; if it is firm like the tip of your nose, it is medium; and if it is slightly firmer like your forehead, it is well done.)

3. Meanwhile, increase the heat of the oil for the chips to 190°C/375°F, then return the precooked chips in batches to the fryer and cook for 5 minutes, or until golden brown and crisp. Drain well on kitchen paper and season. Serve the steaks with the chips, Dijon mustard and a salad.

Spiced Lamb with Melting Onions

If time allows, marinate the lamb overnight to add flavour and tenderize the meat.

Preparation time: 5 minutes, plus overnight marinating (optional) • Cooking time: 15 minutes • 315 calories per serving • Serves 4

What you need

1 lemon • 350g (12oz) onions, thickly sliced • ½ tsp ground cumin • ¾ tsp salt • 60ml (4 tbsp) olive oil • 450g (1lb) boned leg of lamb, cut into 2.5cm (1in) cubes • cooked basmati rice, to serve • coriander sprigs, to garnish

What to do

1. Squeeze the lemon, then cut it into quarters. Mix the lemon quarters, 45ml (3 tbsp) lemon juice, onions, ground cumin, salt and olive oil in a shallow dish. Add the lamb and turn to coat it well in the onion and lemon marinade. If you have enough time, cover the dish and leave the lamb to marinate overnight in the refrigerator.

2. Place the onion and lemon marinade in an even layer in the bottom of a grill pan and sprinkle with 30ml (2 tbsp) water.

3. Heat the grill to high and place the lamb in the pan, about 5cm (2in) away from the heat. Grill for 15 minutes, until the lamb is well charred but still pink in the middle, and the onions are soft and golden. Stir the mixture with a wooden spoon as it cooks. Some liquid will come out of the lamb and onions and this needs to evaporate before the lamb browns. Serve the grilled lamb, onions and lemons on a bed of basmati rice. Garnish with coriander sprigs.

Crispy Pork with Fennel and Apple

A fatty cut of pork, such as streaky slices, belly pork or spare ribs lends the best flavour to this dish, complementing the apples and honey.

Preparation time: 15 minutes • Cooking time: 1 hour, 20 minutes • 507 calories per serving • Serves 4

What you need

30ml (2 tbsp) dark soy sauce • 1 tbsp runny honey • 700g (1½lb) pork streaky slices or thick slices of belly pork • salt and freshly ground black pepper • 550g (1lb 4oz) Granny Smith apples, peeled, cored and finely diced • 1 tbsp fennel seeds • 1 garlic clove, sliced • 45ml (3 tbsp) oil

What to do

1. Preheat the oven to 200°C/400°F/Gas Mark 6. Mix together the soy sauce and honey in a roasting tin, add the pork and turn to coat well. Arrange the pork skin-side up and season well, making sure the fat is well salted (this helps to make the crackling crisp). Roast for 40 minutes, turning the pork from time to time.

2. Mix together the apples, fennel, garlic and oil, then spoon around the pork in an even layer. Roast the pork for a further 40 minutes, or until the meat is golden and tender, and the fat is crisp. (The apple will have softened and turned a deep golden colour.) Serve immediately.

Crispy Pork with Fennel and Apple

Greek Lamb and Feta Layer

This dish is based on the Greek classic, moussaka, but topped with creamy yogurt, eggs and Parmesan instead of béchamel sauce.

Preparation time: 20 minutes • Cooking time: 1 hour, 50 minutes • 650 calories per serving • Serves 8

What you need

75ml (5 tbsp) olive oil • 1 large onion, finely chopped • 900g (2lb) lamb mince • 2 garlic cloves, crushed • 2 tbsp tomato purée • 2 x 400g (14oz) cans plum tomatoes in tomato juice • 45ml (3 tbsp) Worcestershire sauce • 2 tbsp chopped fresh oregano • salt and freshly ground black pepper • 3 large potatoes, about 1kg (2¼lb) total weight, scrubbed • 2 large aubergines, trimmed and cut into 5mm (¼in) slices • 2 x 500g (1lb 2oz) tubs Greek yogurt • 4 large eggs • 50g (2oz) Parmesan cheese, freshly grated • pinch of grated nutmeg • 200g (7oz) packet feta cheese, crumbled

What to do

1. Heat 30ml (2 tbsp) of the oil in a large saucepan. Add the onion and cook over a low heat for 10 minutes, or until softened.

2. Put the mince in a large non-stick frying pan and cook for 10–15 minutes over a high heat, breaking up the mince with the back of a spoon, until any liquid has evaporated and the lamb has browned. Add the garlic and tomato purée and cook for a further 2 minutes.

3. Add the lamb mixture to the cooked onion with the tomatoes, Worcestershire sauce and oregano. Bring to the boil, season, then reduce the heat and simmer for 30–40 minutes, until the lamb is tender.

4. Meanwhile, cook the potatoes in boiling salted water for 20–30 minutes, until tender, then drain. Leave to cool, then peel and slice thickly.

5. Brush the aubergine slices with the remaining oil. Preheat two non-stick frying pans and cook the aubergine slices for 2–3 minutes on each side until tender.

6. Mix together the yogurt, eggs and half the Parmesan; season the mixture, then add the nutmeg.

7. Preheat the oven to 180°C/350°F/Gas Mark 4. Divide the lamb between two 1.4 litre (2½ pint) ovenproof dishes or eight individual ovenproof serving dishes. Layer the potatoes, feta and aubergines on top. Spoon the yogurt sauce over the top and sprinkle with the rest of the Parmesan. Bake for 35–40 minutes, until browned.

Pork with Rosemary

This dish couldn't be easier to make but try to use the best-quality meat you can afford.

Preparation time: 10 minutes • Cooking time: 7 minutes • 290 calories per serving • Serves 2

What you need

200g (7oz) pork fillet • 25g (1oz) butter • 150ml (¼ pint) medium-dry white wine • 2 tsp finely chopped fresh rosemary • salt and freshly ground black pepper

What to do

1. Cover the pork fillet with clingfilm and flatten with a heavy pan or rolling pin. Cut into thick diagonal slices.

2. Melt the butter in a frying pan, preferably ridged, add the pork and cook over a high heat until golden brown. Remove from the pan, set aside and keep warm.

3. Add the white wine to the pan, bring to the boil and allow to bubble for 2–3 minutes, until the liquid has reduced by at least half. Add the chopped rosemary and return the pork to the pan. Stir, season and serve.

Braised Sausages with Lentils

Splash out on good-quality organic sausages and serve with mash and green vegetables.

Preparation time: 10 minutes • Cooking time: 30 minutes • 530 calories per serving • Serves 4

What you need

450g (1lb) good-quality sausages • oil, if necessary • 2 red onions, finely chopped • 6 baby red peppers, halved and deseeded, or 2 large peppers, deseeded and thickly sliced • 150ml (¼ pint) light stock • 200ml (7fl oz) red wine • 425g (15oz) can green lentils, drained and rinsed • salt and freshly ground black pepper • chopped fresh parsley, to garnish

What to do

1. Brown the sausages in a large flameproof casserole for 4–5 minutes. (If they do not produce enough fat and begin to stick, add a tablespoon of oil to the pan).
2. Add the onions to the pan; fry for 7 minutes, or until softened. Add the peppers and fry until slightly browned.
3. Add the stock and red wine, bring to the boil and allow the mixture to bubble for 2 minutes. Stir the lentils into the casserole, season and cover tightly, then simmer gently for 15 minutes, or until most of the liquid has been absorbed and the peppers are quite soft. Garnish with parsley to serve.

Greek Lamb and Feta Layer

poultry recipes

Turkey and Roasted Vegetables with Focaccia

Roasting lends a delicious sweetness to the red onions, peppers and tomatoes, and they make a sumptuous topping on focaccia or ciabatta.

Preparation time: 30 minutes • Cooking time: 1 hour, 10 minutes • 400 calories per serving • Serves 6

What you need

900g (2lb) red onions, quartered and separated into 'petals' • 150ml (¼ pint) olive oil • 3 red and 3 yellow peppers, halved, deseeded and cut into wedges • 6 large garlic cloves, unpeeled • 200g (7oz) cherry tomatoes • 30ml (2 tbsp) balsamic vinegar • sea salt flakes and freshly ground black pepper • 30ml (2 tbsp) white wine vinegar • 1 Italian loaf, such as focaccia or ciabatta, thickly sliced • 300g (11oz) cooked turkey, cut into thick strips • basil sprigs and crushed black peppercorns, to garnish

What to do

1. Preheat the oven to 220°C/425°F/Gas Mark 7. Place the red onions in a large roasting tin and toss in 30ml (2 tbsp) of the olive oil. Roast for 10 minutes, then add the peppers and garlic cloves. Mix together thoroughly and return to the oven for 50 minutes, or until the vegetables have charred and softened.
2. Add the tomatoes to the tin and return to the oven for 10 minutes. Remove from the oven, mix in the balsamic vinegar and seasoning. Set aside and keep warm.
3. Pour the white wine vinegar and 90ml (6 tbsp) of the olive oil into a small bowl, then season and whisk thoroughly to make a dressing. Set aside.

4. Toast the slices of focaccia on one side, turn and brush the other side with the remaining oil and toast until brown and crisp. Sprinkle with sea salt flakes.
5. Add the cooked turkey strips to the warm vegetables, then toss in the dressing. Garnish with basil and crushed peppercorns and serve immediately with the focaccia.

Roast Lemon Chicken

What could be simpler than potatoes, garlic and onions roasted with a lemon-infused organic chicken? Serve with vegetables or a salad.

Preparation time: 15 minutes, plus 10 minutes resting • Cooking time: 1 hour, 20 minutes • 676 calories per serving • Serves 4

What you need

900g (2lb) whole chicken • 30ml (2 tbsp) olive oil • sea salt flakes and freshly ground black pepper • 2 lemons • 150ml (¼ pint) dry white wine • 5 garlic cloves, unpeeled 4 potatoes, scrubbed and cut into wedges • 2 tbsp chopped fresh thyme • 2 onions, quartered

What to do

1. Rub the chicken with the oil and seasoning, then place four thick slices of lemon between the skin and the breast of the chicken. Squeeze the remaining lemon and pour the juice over the chicken, then put the used lemon halves inside the body cavity.
2. Preheat the oven to 200°C/400°F/Gas Mark 6. Place the chicken in a roasting tin, breast-side up, with the wine, 150ml (¼ pint) water, the garlic cloves and potatoes. Sprinkle the chicken with the thyme.

3. Roast the chicken for 20 minutes. Turn the chicken over, add the onions to the potatoes and cook for a further 1 hour, or until the juices run clear when the thigh joint is pierced with a sharp knife. Allow the chicken to rest in a warm place for 5–10 minutes before carving.

Chargrilled Chicken with Tomato Compôte

Organic, free-range chickens are known for their superior flavour and texture. Here, the breasts are griddled to give a smoky taste.

Preparation time: 20 minutes • Cooking time: 30 minutes • 420 calories per serving • Serves 4

What you need

salt and freshly ground black pepper • 4 chicken breasts, with skin • 60ml (4 tbsp) olive oil • 12 large asparagus tips • 2 shallots, finely chopped • 6 plum tomatoes, deseeded and finely chopped • 2 tbsp chopped fresh tarragon

What to do

1. Season the chicken. Heat 30ml (1 tbsp) of the oil in a griddle or frying pan, add the chicken and cook for 20–30 minutes, turning half-way through.
2. Heat 30ml (1 tbsp) of the oil in a second pan and fry the asparagus tips for 6–8 minutes, until tender.
3. To make the tomato compôte, heat the remaining oil in another pan, add the shallots and cook for 5 minutes, or until softened. Add the tomatoes and heat through for 1 minute, then stir in the tarragon.
4. Serve the chicken with the asparagus and the compôte.

Roast Lemon Chicken

Glazed Duck with Rosemary

Zesty Orange, Chicken and Tarragon Salad

The smoked chicken breast gives this tangy salad an inspiring twist but if you have trouble finding an organic smoked bird, opt for unsmoked instead.

Preparation time: 15 minutes, plus at least 1 hour chilling • 625 calories per serving • Serves 4

What you need

350g (12oz) smoked chicken or cooked chicken breast, skinned and cut into long strips • 2 large heads of chicory, roughly sliced • 2 oranges, peeled and thickly sliced • 50g (2oz) pecan nuts or walnuts, toasted and roughly chopped • tarragon sprigs, to garnish • **For the orange dressing:** grated rind and juice of 2 oranges • 30ml (2 tbsp) white wine vinegar • 1 tsp caster sugar • salt and freshly ground black pepper • 75ml (5 tbsp) olive oil • 3 tbsp chopped fresh tarragon • 1 large egg yolk

What to do

1. To make the dressing, combine all the dressing ingredients together in a small bowl and mix well.
2. To make the salad, place the chicken in a bowl, spoon over the dressing, cover and chill for at least 1 hour.
3. Place a layer of chicory in a large, flat dish. Spoon the chicken and dressing over the chicory. Scatter over the orange slices and nuts and garnish with tarragon sprigs.

Glazed Duck with Rosemary

Marinated and honey-glazed duck breasts are cooked together with root vegetables for a convenient 'one-pot' Sunday lunch.

Preparation time: 20 minutes, plus 1 hour marinating • Cooking time: 1 hour • 660 calories per serving • Serves 4

What you need

4 duck breasts, about 700g (1½lb) total weight • finely grated rind and juice of 1 lemon • 1 garlic clove, crushed • sea salt and freshly ground black pepper • 450g (1lb) new potatoes, scrubbed and halved • 125g (4oz) shallots, covered with boiling water for 5 minutes, then peeled and halved if large • 225g (8oz) baby leeks, trimmed, or regular leeks cut into 7.5cm (3in) pieces • 225g (8oz) small carrots, halved lengthways • 30ml (2 tbsp) olive oil • 2 tbsp chopped fresh rosemary • 4 tsp runny honey • rosemary sprigs, to garnish

What to do

1. Score the skin of the duck breasts with a sharp knife. Put the lemon rind and juice, garlic and seasoning in a shallow ceramic dish. Add the duck breasts in a single layer, turn several times to coat them in the marinade and refrigerate for 1 hour to allow the flavours to mingle.

2. Preheat the oven to 220°C/425°F/Gas Mark 7. Place the prepared potatoes, shallots, leeks and carrots together in a large roasting tin. Toss the vegetables in the oil, then sprinkle with sea salt and chopped rosemary. Roast for 30 minutes.

3. Arrange the duck breasts on a metal rack that will fit over the roasting tin. Smear the duck skin with the honey and sprinkle generously with sea salt. Remove the vegetables from the oven and turn, draining off any oil. Position the duck on the rack over the vegetables and roast for 25–30 minutes, until the duck has browned and is tender and the vegetables are a little charred.

Sticky Baked Sesame Chicken

Marmalade makes an unusual base for this oriental-inspired marinade. Serve the chicken with boiled rice, noodles or potato wedges.

Preparation time: 5 minutes, plus 15 minutes marinating • Cooking time: 35 minutes • 140 calories per serving • Serves 4

What you need

2 garlic cloves, finely chopped • 2.5cm (1in) piece of fresh root ginger, peeled and finely chopped • 3 tbsp orange marmalade • 45ml (3 tbsp) dark soy sauce • 8 chicken thighs, with skin • 2 tbsp sesame seeds, to garnish • cooked white rice, to serve

What to do

1. Preheat the oven to 220°C/425°F/Gas Mark 7. Mix together the garlic, ginger, marmalade and soy sauce in a large bowl. Add the chicken thighs, stir, cover and set aside for 15 minutes.

2. Place the chicken in a roasting tin and roast for 35 minutes, basting and turning the chicken so that it cooks evenly and is cooked to the centre. Lift the chicken out of the tin and keep warm.

3. Skim off the fat in the roasting tin and discard. Bring the juices to the boil and allow to bubble for 30 seconds. Spoon the juices over the chicken, sprinkle with sesame seeds and serve.

Steam-Grilled Oriental Salmon

fish
recipes

Warm Salmon with Mango and Dill Salsa

Quick and easy to make, yet impressive, too, the sharpness of the salsa cuts through the richness of the salmon fillets.

Preparation time: 10 minutes • Cooking time: 10 minutes • 390 calories per serving • Serves 4

What you need

30ml (2 tbsp) olive oil • 4 salmon fillets, about 175g (6oz) each • boiled new potatoes, to serve • dill sprigs, to garnish • **For the salsa:** 1 large mango, peeled, stoned and diced • 1 large red chilli, deseeded and finely chopped • 30ml (2 tbsp) lime juice • 2 tbsp chopped fresh dill, plus sprigs to garnish

What to do

1. To make the salsa, put the mango in a bowl with the chilli, lime juice and dill, and toss together.

2. Heat the olive oil in a non-stick frying pan and add the salmon fillets. Cook for 6–10 minutes (depending on the thickness of the fillets), turning them half-way through, until just cooked.

3. Serve the salmon with a mound of mango salsa and boiled new potatoes, garnished with dill sprigs.

Seared Salmon with Lime Dressing

Salmon is one of the very few types of fish that can be bought as organic. It has a superior flavour and texture and is great served simply, as here.

Preparation time: 20 minutes • Cooking time: 12 minutes • 390 calories per serving • Serves 4

What you need

4 thick salmon fillets, about 125g (4oz) each • 4 tsp sea-weed salt (2 tsp crushed sea salt mixed with 2 tsp mixed crushed peppercorns) • 3 limes • 2 small fennel bulbs, sliced • 2 x 100g (3½ oz) packets asparagus tips • 150g (5oz) courgettes, cut into batons • 15ml (1 tbsp) olive oil • 1 red onion, sliced • 45ml (3 tbsp) extra-virgin olive oil

What to do

1. Place the salmon fillets in a shallow dish. Sprinkle the seaweed salt and the grated rind and juice of one lime over the salmon.

2. Heat a non-stick griddle pan until really hot. Cook the salmon for 2 minutes on each side to sear, then for a further 2 minutes on each side to cook through.

3. Bring a large saucepan of salted water to the boil, add the juice of half a lime, the fennel, asparagus and cour-gettes. Bring to the boil, cook for 3 minutes, then drain.

4. Remove the salmon from the griddle pan and keep warm in a moderate oven. Add the olive oil and red onion to the pan, cook for 1 minute, then squeeze in the juice of half a lime. Add the fennel, asparagus and courgettes to the pan and stir-fry for a couple of minutes.

5. Whisk together the extra-virgin olive oil and the grated rind and juice of the remaining lime. Drizzle the dressing over the salmon and serve with the vegetables.

Steam-Grilled Oriental Salmon

Cooking salmon in a 'parcel' helps to retain valuable moisture and nutrients in the fish.

Preparation time: 15 minutes • Cooking time: 10 minutes • 300 calories per serving • Serves 4

What you need

sesame oil, for greasing • 4 salmon fillets, about 150g (5oz) x 2.5cm (1in) thick each • 60ml (4 tbsp) soy sauce • 200g (7oz) pak choi or spinach • 2.5cm (1in) piece of fresh root ginger, peeled and coarsely grated • 4 spring onions, sliced • coriander sprigs, to garnish • cooked Thai rice, to serve

What to do

1. Lightly grease four large sheets of foil, each about 35cm (14in) square, with sesame oil. Place a salmon fillet in the centre of each piece of foil and drizzle each with 15ml (1 tbsp) of the soy sauce.

2. Divide the pak choi, ginger and spring onions between the salmon fillets and fold up the foil loosely but neatly to form parcels. Seal the edges well so the parcels can be turned over during cooking. (Make sure the foil parcels are large enough to allow for the expansion of air that takes place as the salmon begins to cook.)

3. Place the parcels under a hot grill (or barbecue) and cook for 4–5 minutes on each side. Serve the sealed parcels to your guests at the table – warn them to take care as they open the parcels as the steam builds up inside. Garnish with coriander sprigs and serve with fragrant Thai rice.

Salmon with Spring Onion Noodles

This oriental-flavoured dish is equally delicious served cold as a main course salad.

Preparation time: 15 minutes • Cooking time: 20 minutes • 595 calories per serving • Serves 4

What you need

45ml (3 tbsp) dark soy sauce • 4 tbsp caster sugar • juice of 1 lime • 75ml (5 tbsp) sunflower oil • 125g (4oz) egg thread noodles • 4 skinless salmon fillets, about 150g (5oz) each • salt and freshly ground black pepper • 4 tsp Chinese five-spice powder • 125g (4oz) spring onions, cut into thin strips • 125g (4oz) celery, cut into thin strips • 125g (4oz) cucumber, halved lengthways, deseeded, and cut into thin strips • coriander sprigs, to garnish

What to do

1. Place the soy sauce and sugar in a small saucepan, bring to the boil then remove from the heat. Stir in the lime juice and 60ml (4 tbsp) of the oil, then set aside.

2. Roughly break the noodles and place in a bowl. Cover with boiling water, soak for 4 minutes, then rinse and drain well.

3. Season each salmon fillet with salt, pepper and 1 tsp Chinese five-spice powder. Heat the remaining oil in a large non-stick frying pan, add the salmon and cook for 4 minutes on each side.

4. Toss the drained noodles in the soy sauce dressing with the spring onions, celery and cucumber. Arrange the noodles on individual plates, top with the salmon and garnish with coriander sprigs.

Salmon with Couscous

This Moroccan-inspired main-course salad combines broad beans, limes, spring onions and mint with grilled salmon and fluffy grains of couscous.

Preparation time: 15 minutes, plus 10 minutes soaking • Cooking time: 20 minutes • 593 calories per serving • Serves 4

What you need

225g (8oz) frozen broad beans • salt and freshly ground black pepper • 250g (9oz) couscous • 60ml (4 tbsp) olive oil • 4 thick salmon fillets, skinned, about 150g (5oz) each • juice and grated rind of 2 limes • 4 spring onions, finely sliced • 3 tbsp chopped fresh mint, plus extra to garnish

What to do

1. Cook the beans in boiling salted water for 5–10 minutes, drain and set aside. Place the couscous in a bowl with ½ tsp salt, then add 300ml (½ pint) boiling water and 15ml (1 tbsp) of the olive oil. Stir well, cover and leave to soak for 10 minutes.

2. Meanwhile, season the salmon fillets and grill for 5 minutes on each side or until just cooked to the centre. Set aside to cool slightly.

3. Fluff up the couscous with a fork, add the lime juice, spring onions, mint and remaining oil. Season well.

4. Flake the salmon and gently fold it into the couscous salad with the broad beans. Garnish with chopped fresh mint and the grated lime rind, and serve.

Salt-Crusted Trout with Tarragon and Garlic

Organic trout is becoming increasingly available. Here, its moist texture and subtle flavour is retained by the salt crust.

Preparation time: 10 minutes • Cooking time: 20 minutes • 252 calories per serving • Serves 6

What you need

about 900g (2lb) sea salt • 6 tbsp chopped fresh tarragon • 6–8 garlic cloves, unpeeled • 6 trout, heads and tails removed, if preferred • lemon wedges, to garnish

What to do

1. Preheat the oven to 220°C/425°F/Gas Mark 7. Line a roasting tin with foil and add enough salt to make a 1cm (½in) layer. Scatter half the tarragon over the salt and add the unpeeled garlic cloves.

2. Press the trout into the salt, scatter over the remaining tarragon, then cover completely with more salt.

3. Bake the trout for 20 minutes, or until cooked. Serve the trout in its salty jacket or remove the salt and skin beforehand. Garnish with wedges of lemon.

Salmon with Couscous

flour and baked goods

Grains play a starring role in a healthy diet. From the mainstay of bread, through breakfast cereals to the occasional pleasures of sweet desserts, cakes, pastries and biscuits, for most of us a meal or even a snack is never quite satisfying without them. They are important providers of energy – giving carbohydrates, protein and fibre, as well as essential vitamins and minerals.

Worldwide variety

Grains have always been a vital part of every culture's diet. Historically, different parts of the world relied on whatever grain was best suited to a particular climate. All except buckwheat are varieties of cultivated grasses and they were among the earliest foods eaten by humans. Rye, oats and buckwheat grew well in colder parts of the globe; wheat, barley and millet in more temperate zones; maize in the New World and rice in the Far East. Many of the animals we eat are fed on grains, too. The range of foods made from grains is huge – breads, pastas, noodles, cakes, biscuits and pastries are a feature of every food culture.

Organic differences

The best way to convince yourself to buy organic is to compare the taste and texture of organic and non-organic bread. Nowadays, there is a huge choice of organic breads from all over the world, as well as staple wholemeal stoneground loaves. Environmentally of course there should be no question about buying organic grains since

the conventional methods of producing grain crops are destructive to the soil and eco-systems, relying heavily on chemical inputs – including organophosphates and the ozone-depleter, methyl bromide – both during the growing period and after harvesting. The frequent applications of herbicides have a disastrous effect on wildlife and are just as important an issue as pesticide residues in the food we ourselves consume. Organic cereal fields support a much more diverse range of rare plant species, bugs and birds.

Brown or white?

Soft white bread, made from grain milled into flour and then sifted through finer and finer sieves until the nutritious, brown, outer husk of the grain is finally left behind, has been highly prized since ancient times. Because the process of refining flour was so expensive most people couldn't afford the luxury of snowy white bread and fine pastry. Because their diet was limited by economics, the foods they could afford, such as hearty bread full of goodness, was an important part of the ordinary citizen's diet. With the Industrial Revolution it became possible for flour to be milled inexpensively and white bread could be mass produced. Everyone could then indulge in this whiteness, even those at the bottom of the economic scale for whom it had previously been beyond their means. The popularity of white bread is probably in part still because of this former association with status and rank.

Best choice

The best choice for anyone seriously interested in eating real bread is to look for the words 'organic' and 'stone-ground'. Mill stones powered by running water or electricity leave most of the nutritious bran in the flour; slightly more is milled out when the flour is processed through high-powered metal rolling mills, even in the manufacture of wholemeal flour. A well-made, stoneground wholemeal loaf should feel quite weighty when you pick it up. Mass-produced commercial versions are very different. These are made with refined flour, flour improvers and chemicals to keep them 'fresh' longer.

Versatile starches

Anyone who cooks a lot will probably use a number of different flours. Any grain can be ground into flour but they are all best freshly ground as they lose their flavour and develop a stale musty smell if kept for too long. They are also susceptible to insect infestation and should always be kept in dry, sealed containers.

Finely ground corn flour, sometimes called corn starch, potato and rice flours are most often used for thickening sauces and soups and occasionally in biscuit-making. Coarser corn meal and polenta (the Italian variety) are often used as an alternative to wheat flour for coating foods to be fried, and are made into a variety of savoury porridge and breads in South America and the Caribbean. Native Americans used amaranth flour as a staple for thousands of years; this is now increasingly available and also makes delicious nutritious savoury dishes. Also watch

Organic flour types

Nowadays there is a huge range of organic flours readily available – most cooks will probably use a variety of different flours. For supplier information, see *Organic Directory*

Type   Uses

Amaranth flour dishes   versatile, good for savoury

Barley flour   low gluten. Excellent for breads and scones, for thickening milk-based sauces

Buckwheat flour   gluten-free, strong flavour. good for breads and pastries and dumplings. Used to make blinis, pancakes, muffins and crumpets.

Corn flour (corn starch)   good for thickening sauces, soups, for making biscuits.

Corn meal (polenta)   alternative to wheat flour, for coating foods to be fried and for savoury porridges.

Blue cornmeal   for tortillas and pancakes.

Gram flour (chickpea flour)   used in Mediterranean and Asian cooking, for making breads and as a coating and thickening agent.

Malted flour   brown flour with nutty taste, for breads and speciality cakes.

Millet flour   gluten-free, good for breads and pastries and dumplings and toppings for stews and casseroles and thickening sauces.

Oatmeal   excellent for biscuits, such as oatcakes and for thickening sauces and soups. Available in several grades from the coarsest – pinhead – to rough, medium, fine and superfine.

Potato flour   gluten-free. Usually mixed with wheat flour in recipes for cakes and scones. Excellent for thickening sauces and soups.

Rice flour   similar to semolina, good for thickening milk-based sauces and puddings and in cakes and biscuits.

Rye flour (light and dark)   deliciously nutty, especially good for dark breads.

Semolina   high protein and gluten content. Used to make gnocchi and special breads, sometimes mixed with flour to make pasta.

Spelt flour   good for bread, cakes, pizzas and other baked goods.

Stoneground flour   flour that has been ground in traditional way, between stones to give better flavour.

Wheat flour (wholewheat)   versatile: good for sauces, baking and coating foods.

Wholemeal flour   versatile: good for all types of (fine brown flour)baking, in cooking and for thickening.

White flour and   unbleached white flour for lighter cakes (sponges and small cakes) and pastry for bread and as a thickening agent, for dusting and

---

out for flours made from legumes rather than grains. Gram flour, made from chickpeas, is extremely nutritious and there are a number of delicious ways to use it in cuisines as diverse as those from the Mediterranean and Asia. It can also be used for coating and thickening.

Wheat is made into various types of flours that are used for breads, pasta, cakes and pastries. Most cooks will use both wholemeal and unbleached white flours as well as finely ground flours for pastry, and more robust flours for breads. Millet and buckwheat flours are gluten-free, and rye flour is useful for making dark, European-style breads.

Storing bread

Most fresh breads should keep for several days in a cool dry container. People have their personal favourites, from wooden bins to earthenware crocks, but bread will keep just as well in a sealed bag in the refrigerator. Some specialist and unleavened breads are best eaten fresh rather than being stored. Stale bread can be whizzed into breadcrumbs in a food processor or grated, then stored in the refrigerator in a screw-top jar or air-tight plastic container – ready to use in cooking.

Healthy start

Most breakfast cereals, even some of the organic ones, contain a lot of sugar and other sweeteners. If you want to avoid this extra sugar, organic porridge oats and muesli are a good alternative. In China, rice porridge is eaten at breakfast and there are a number of organic brown rice cereals available. Organic polenta (ground maize) can also be made into a quick breakfast porridge by stirring three tablespoons of polenta and a pinch of sea salt into a cup of boiling water, which will cook in five to eight minutes. Buckwheat groats (kasha) or cracked wheat (burgul or bulgur) can also be cooked quite quickly with a little broth or plain water. The addition of a few sultanas or currants provides natural sweetness.

Noodles and pasta

There is a splendid variety of organic noodles and pastas on the market and an excellent range of organic pasta sauces. Brown pasta is something of an acquired taste but it you haven't already sampled it, give it a try. It is slightly weighty but has a robust flavour. Try making your own pasta with organic brown flour, or use organic white for a lighter result. There are also many organic gluten-free pastas on the market.

Baked goods

The sweet-toothed are catered for by a bountiful selection of cakes, biscuits and puddings made with organic ingredients. But even if you have a very busy lifestyle it can take only minutes to make many simple treats yourself, such as biscuits or pancakes; or indulge yourself and spend longer making a special meal – after all, part of living organic should be the enjoyment of preparing treats for yourself and your family.

baking recipes

Carrot and Orange Squares

Moist and light, this cake is topped with a rich layer of slightly sweetened cream cheese.

Preparation time: 15 minutes, plus cooling •
Cooking time: 40 minutes • 450 calories per square •
Makes 12 squares

What you need

butter, for greasing • 250ml (8fl oz) sunflower oil • 225g (8oz) caster sugar • 3 large eggs • 225g (8oz) self-raising flour, sifted • pinch of salt • 250g (9oz) carrots, coarsely grated • 1 tsp orange flower water (optional) • **For the icing:** 50g (2oz) butter, preferably unsalted • 200g (7oz) packet cream cheese • 40g (1½oz) icing sugar, sifted • grated rind of 2 oranges and 30ml (2 tbsp) juice

What to do

1. Preheat the oven to 180°C/350°F/Gas Mark 4. Grease and line the base of an 18 x 28cm (7 x 11in) x 2.5cm (1in) deep tin. Whisk the oil and sugar together, then whisk in the eggs one at a time. Gently fold in the flour and salt, then the carrots and orange flower water, if using.
2. Pour the mixture into the prepared tin and bake for 40 minutes, or until golden and risen. Insert a skewer into the middle of the cake – if it comes out clean the cake is cooked. Leave in the tin for 10 minutes, then turn out on to a wire rack to cool.
3. To make the icing, beat together the butter and cream cheese until light and fluffy. Beat in the icing sugar, half the grated orange rind and the juice.
4. When the cake is cool, remove the lining paper. Spread the cake with a 5mm (¼in) layer of icing; decorate with the remaining orange rind. Cut into twelve squares to serve.

Quick Gooey Chocolate Puddings

Rich, gooey and totally indulgent, serve these puddings warm with cream or ice cream. Organic chocolate is now widely available.

Preparation time: 10 minutes • Cooking time: 20 minutes
• 475 calories per pudding • Makes 4

What you need

100g (3½oz) good-quality dark chocolate with 70 per cent cocoa solids • 100g (3½oz) butter, plus extra for greasing • 2 large eggs • 100g (3½oz) caster sugar, plus extra for 'lining' • 20g (¾oz) plain flour • icing sugar, to decorate

What to do

1. Preheat the oven to 200°C/400°F/Gas Mark 6. Melt the chocolate and butter together in a heatproof bowl, placed over a pan of gently simmering water. Allow to cool.
2. Whisk together the eggs, sugar and flour. Combine the chocolate and egg mixtures and spoon into four buttered and sugared 200ml (7fl oz) ramekins.
3. Place the ramekins on a baking tray and bake for 12–15 minutes, until the puddings have risen and are firm on the outside but runny inside. Turn out, dust with icing sugar and serve.

Apple and Blueberry Cake

Organic apples and blueberries add a juiciness to this teatime cake, which also makes a perfect dessert served warm with cream.

Preparation time: 20 minutes, plus cooling • Cooking time: 1 hour • 390 calories per slice • Makes 8 slices

What you need

125g (4oz) chilled butter, diced, plus extra for greasing • 225g (8oz) self-raising flour, sifted • ½ tsp salt • 175g (6oz) granulated sugar, preferably golden • 2 large eggs, beaten • 2 large Granny Smith apples, peeled, cored and sliced • 125g (4oz) blueberries • 175g (6oz) apricot jam • 15ml (1 tbsp) lemon juice

What to do

1. Preheat the oven to 190°C/375°F/Gas Mark 5. Grease and line the base of a 20cm (8in) spring-form tin with non-stick parchment paper.

2. Put the flour and salt in a large mixing bowl. Add the diced butter and rub it into the flour until the mixture resembles fine breadcrumbs. Add 125g (4oz) of the sugar with the beaten eggs, and stir well.

3. Spread half the cake mixture in a thin layer in the tin, then layer the apples and blueberries over the top, reserving a little of the fruit for the top of the cake. Sprinkle with the remaining sugar, then spoon in the rest of the cake mixture. Add the remaining apple slices and blueberries, pressing them down slightly into the mixture.

4. Bake for 45–55 minutes, until risen and firm to the touch. Insert a skewer into the middle of the cake – if it comes out clean the cake is cooked. Leave in the tin for 10 minutes, then turn out on to a wire rack to cool.

5. Warm the jam and lemon juice in a small saucepan until melted and combined. Sieve the mixture and, while it is still warm, brush it over the top of the cake. Serve the cake immediately.

Carrot and Orange Squares

Quick Courgette, Lemon and Parmesan Bread

Quick Courgette, Lemon and Parmesan Bread

This bread-cum-savoury cake is a good way of using up surplus or leftover vegetables. Parsnips and carrots can be substituted for the courgettes.

Preparation time: 25 minutes, plus cooling • Cooking time: 50 minutes • 171 calories per serving • Makes 12 slices

What you need

butter, for greasing • 175g (6oz) plain flour, sifted, plus extra for dusting • 175g (6oz) courgettes, coarsely grated • 75g (3oz) wholemeal flour • 1 tbsp caster sugar • 1 tbsp baking powder • ½ tsp salt • finely grated rind of 1 lemon • 75g (3oz) Parmesan cheese, freshly grated, plus extra for sprinkling • freshly ground black pepper • 200ml (7fl oz) milk • 75ml (5 tbsp) olive oil • 2 medium eggs, beaten

What to do

1. Preheat the oven to 190°C/375°F/Gas Mark 5. Grease and line the base of a 900g (2lb) non-stick loaf tin and dust with flour. Dry the courgettes well on kitchen paper.
2. Place the flours, sugar, baking powder, salt and lemon rind in a bowl and mix well. Add the courgettes, the Parmesan and black pepper and mix lightly with a fork. Make a well in the centre. Whisk together the milk, oil and eggs and pour into the well, stirring until smooth.
3. Pour the mixture into the tin and level the surface. Bake for 50 minutes, or until a skewer inserted into the centre of the loaf comes out clean. Leave in the tin for 10 minutes, turn out on a wire rack. Sprinkle with Parmesan once cool.

Simple Brown Loaf

A straightforward, light and wholesome loaf, which is great toasted and spread with butter.

Preparation time: 25 minutes, plus 20 minutes sponging and 3 hours rising • Cooking time: 1 hour • 1,651 calories per loaf • Makes 900g (2lb) loaf

What you need

300g (11oz) strong white flour, sifted • 200g (7oz) strong wholemeal flour • 1 tsp dried or 15g (½oz) fresh yeast, crumbled • 2 tsp salt • oil, for greasing

What to do

1. Put the flours in a large bowl, make a well in the centre and pour in 325ml (11fl oz) tepid water.

2. Sprinkle the yeast over the water, then mix a little of the flour with the water and yeast to form a batter.

3. Sprinkle the salt over the remaining dry flour, making sure it does not come into contact with the yeast. Cover the bowl with a clean tea towel and leave for 20 minutes.

4. Combine the flour and salt with the batter to make a soft dough and knead for 10 minutes. When the dough feels smooth and elastic, shape it into a ball. Place it in a lightly oiled bowl, cover with a tea towel, and leave to rise for 45 minutes–1½ hours, until doubled in size. (The longer a dough takes to rise, the more interesting its flavour. Do not rush the process by putting it in a really warm place – cool to normal room temperatures are best).

5. When the dough has risen, knock it back by pressing down with your knuckles to expel any air. Knead briefly, shape the loaf and put it in a well-greased 900g (2lb) loaf tin or on a lightly floured baking tray. Cover the dough and leave to rise for a further 45 minutes–1½ hours, until doubled in size and spongy.

6. Meanwhile, preheat the oven to 200°C/400°F/Gas Mark 6. Bake the loaf for 50–60 minutes in a tin, or 45–50 minutes on a baking tray. To check the bread is done, tap the bottom and listen for a hollow sound. Allow to cool on a wire rack before serving.

Fruit Scones

These scones are great with home-made jam and fresh clotted cream.

Preparation time: 15 minutes • Cooking time: 15 minutes • 140 calories per scone • Makes 8

What you need

225g (8oz) self-raising flour, plus extra for dusting • pinch of salt • 1 tsp baking powder • 40g (1½oz) chilled butter, diced, plus extra for greasing • 50g (2oz) currants, sultanas, raisins or chopped dates • 150ml (¼ pint) milk • beaten egg or milk, to glaze

What to do

1. Preheat the oven to 220°C/425°F/Gas Mark 7. Sift the flour, salt and baking powder in a bowl. Rub in the butter until the mixture resembles fine breadcrumbs. Stir in the dried fruit. Mix in enough milk to give a fairly soft dough.

2. Turn out the dough on to a lightly floured surface and lightly roll to a 2cm (¾in) thickness. Cut out eight squares, or rounds, using a 6.5cm (2½in) plain cutter. Reroll the trimmings to make more squares or rounds.

3. Place the scones on a greased baking tray and brush the tops with beaten egg or milk. Bake for about 12–15 minutes, until golden and well risen. Transfer to a wire rack to cool slightly before serving.

the store
cupboard

A well-stocked store cupboard is a treasure trove of really useful staples and flavourings. Almost every ingredient in it can now be found bearing the organic label. From it the canny cook can create exciting dishes with just a handful of fresh ingredients or leftovers. Sensible organization, clear labelling and frequent updating are what makes it work to your advantage.

Guidelines

There are no rigidly fixed rules for keeping order in the store cupboard. You are the one who is going to use it and you make the decisions. The first guideline is not to store food you don't want, or that is past its best. When you think an item may be past its prime, give it the sniff test. Dried herbs and spices with no aroma will not impart much flavour in cooking. Anything that smells stale should be thrown away. Get rid of dented cans that are bulging and jars with rusty lids. Many staples such as rice and noodles keep well but not for ever. Flavourings such as vanilla extract usually contain a little alcohol, which preserves them for a long time, even years.

Containers

Plastic boxes with snap-on covers and glass jars with screw-top lids are not expensive – recycled jars are free – and provide secure storage containers for food that comes in fragile bags or boxes not suitable for long-term storage. If you do leave food in the bags they come in, keep them closed with clothes pegs or plastic clips designed for the

purpose. Food leaks and spills attract insects. Few items benefit from strong sunlight so open shelves are not suitable for storing food unless it is kept in opaque containers. Damp conditions accelerate deterioration even faster than light so make sure all food is adequately sealed. You need some storage areas that are dark, cool and dry, particularly for fresh vegetables, but if you are designing a kitchen from scratch make sure that your darker storage areas are adequately illuminated with electric lights.

Basics at a glance

Every cook has their own individual selection of cooking ingredients that they consider essential – some of them for everyday use, others that are required less often. Most cooks will store extra supplies of sea salt and peppercorns, whole spices such as nutmeg and cinnamon sticks, ground spices and aromatic seeds, vanilla pods and liquid extract, an assortment of sugars and other sweeteners, cooking chocolate and cocoa. It is useful to keep extra supplies of tea, coffee and bottled drinks in reserve, in addition to starchy staples such as breakfast cereals, flours, noodles and pasta, dried yeast and other rising agents for bread- and pastry-making. Ingredients for making soups and stews may include dried and canned tomatoes and tomato purée, bouillon powder, stock cubes and dried mushrooms. For salads, keep a selection of olive and nut oils and plain and flavoured vinegars for dressings. Milder flavoured olive and cold-pressed vegetable oils are basics for cooking, and exotics such as soy sauce, miso and curry pastes are useful store cupboard items, too. A well-rounded store cupboard should also contain relishes, pickles, bottled sauces, savoury and sweet biscuits, ground and whole nuts and dried fruit, which are useful for quick snacks as well as in baking.

Everyone knows what they use most often and, ideally, these items should be the most accessible. If you take sugar with your tea or coffee you don't want to have to scramble blindly at the back of the shelves every time the sugar bowl is empty. If you seldom bake, store flours where you can easily find them but don't waste valuable space at the front of the cupboard for something you use only once or twice a month.

What is it?

Most store cupboards have black holes of mystery items – unidentified lurking jars, cans and bags with no labels. When a bag of gram flour is new and you have made onion bajis with half of it you think you will always remember that it is not buckwheat flour. But wait a month or two and you may discover that you have not the faintest idea where you put it or even exactly what it looks like. Try and take the time to decant food packed in fragile cellophane bags or flimsy boxes into sturdy air-tight plastic containers or glass jars and attach a stick-on label or write on it with a marking pen. It will save you time later as you won't have to puzzle out what things are!

Sweet basics

Our food would taste dull without sweetness. Organic sugars and other sweeteners are widely available, and it is useful to have a good variety in your store cupboard. White and brown sugars made from organic sugar cane or sugar beet are ground to different degrees of fineness. Granulated sugar is the coarsest, the next finest is caster, or superfine, and the finest sugar is icing, or confectioner's. Finer sugar is easier to cream into butter but the difference between granulated and caster is relatively minimal and in fact you can always whizz granulated sugar in a blender or coffee grinder to make it finer – although it will never be as fine as icing sugar.

Dark-brown raw sugars from Demerara and Barbados contain more of the minerals calcium, phosphorous, iron, potassium and sodium, which occur in only minute traces in refined white sugar. Sticky dark blackstrap molasses is made from what is left after white sugar is refined from cane and is claimed to be a good source of iron. Similar in taste to black treacle, it is delicious stirred into yogurt or dribbled on ice cream and is often used in baking. Golden syrup is the light, refined, 'white' version of black treacle. Another liquid sweetener with a more delicate and unusual flavour is maple syrup, made from the sap tapped from sugar maples in North America, which is good used for cooking and on its own. Malt syrup or malt extract, made from corn or barley is almost as sweet as honey; it has an earthy flavour but it is not as commonly used as the other liquid sweeteners.

Honey is the only naturally occurring sweetener. Commercially blended honeys, labelled as the 'produce of more than one country', are bland compared with honey from bees that have fed on a particular flower – chestnut, lavender, pine, clover and so on. Although these honeys are more expensive, they do have a superb flavour. Many beekeepers resort to antibiotics to combat a virus that has afflicted bees throughout the world and their honey may contain traces of it. Organic honey does not. No store cupboard should be without at least one jar of really good honey, for eating and for general health – it is particularly useful to soothe irritated throats and help stave off the misery of a cold.

Salts

If you can, try and get hold of organic 'wet' salt, which is totally unrefined and full of minerals. Otherwise, use sea salt, preferably in crystal form, and avoid salt labelled 'free-flowing' as this often means it contains artificial chemicals – read the label.

Salt is often stored near the cooker but flavoured salts, such as those with ground herbs or sea vegetables, can live in the store cupboard. Soy sauce is the means by which Oriental cooks salt their food; organic varieties and those brewed without wheat, useful for anyone with a sensitivity to gluten, are now widely available. Anointing a piece of meat or a bird to be roasted with a mixture of soy sauce and olive oil using a pastry brush or sprig of rosemary gives it a wonderful crisp brown surface.

Hot drinks

Teas, coffees and herbal brews have fugitive flavours that need to be carefully stored or their flavour will evaporate. Glass jars are attractive but not practical as light is an enemy of flavour. Coffee beans can be frozen but they need to thaw a little before being ground. Drinking chocolate is simply cocoa powder with added sugar. If space is limited, cocoa powder on its own is a more useful store cupboard item since most recipes specify plain unsweetened cocoa. Dark cooking chocolate also makes a luxurious hot drink.

Nuts and seeds

All nuts and seeds are extremely nutritious and useful ingredients for cooking and snacking. They were among the earliest foods consumed by humans and contain the essential fatty oils that are needed for brain development. Nuts are high in calories but are nutrient-dense and valuable sources of protein, calcium and other micro-nutrients. Ground almonds are an exceedingly useful cooking ingredient for both sweet and savoury dishes, but all nuts have a place in the larder. One nut in particular should be eaten every day – most of our flour is now lacking in the important mineral selenium, and all you need can be obtained by eating just one brazil nut a day.

Once any nuts have been shelled the oils they contain will go rancid if they are not properly kept; the refrigerator is usually the best place for them. Because nut allergies are so common, all foods that contain even the smallest trace of nuts must, by law, be labelled. When introducing nuts to young children, it is wise to observe them closely. If a child spits out any food and vomits, begins to choke or develops a rash ring a doctor straight away.

store cupboard
recipes

Mixed Mushroom Risotto

Arborio or other specialist risotto rice is essential for a successful creamy tasting end result.

Preparation time: 10 minutes • Cooking time: 30 minutes • 530 calories per serving • Serves 4

What you need

90ml (6 tbsp) olive oil • 2 shallots, finely chopped • 2 garlic cloves, finely chopped • 2 tsp chopped fresh thyme, plus sprigs to garnish • 1 tsp grated lemon rind • 350g (12oz) arborio rice • 150ml (¼ pint) dry white wine • 900ml (1½ pints) hot vegetable stock • 450g (1lb) mixed fresh mushrooms, such as oyster, shiitake, ceps, sliced if large • 1 tbsp chopped fresh flat-leaf parsley • salt and freshly ground black pepper

What to do

1. Heat half the oil in a heavy-based saucepan. Add the shallots, garlic, thyme and lemon rind; fry for 5 minutes, or until the shallots have softened. Add the rice and stir for 1 minute, until the grains are glossy and coated in oil.
2. Add the white wine, bring to the boil and allow to bubble rapidly until it has almost totally evaporated.
3. Gradually add the hot stock to the rice, a ladleful at a time, allowing each addition to be absorbed before adding more. Continue to add the stock until the rice is tender – this will take about 20 minutes.
4. About 5 minutes before the rice is ready, heat the remaining oil in a large frying pan. Add the mushrooms to the oil and stir-fry over a high heat for 4–5 minutes.

5. Stir the mushrooms into the rice along with the parsley. Season to taste and serve immediately, garnished with thyme sprigs.

Mixed Bean Salad with Lemon Vinaigrette

Canned organic beans are a convenient store cupboard standby, requiring no presoaking or prolonged cooking.

Preparation time: 15 minutes • 289 calories per serving • Serves 6

What you need

400g (14oz) can mixed beans, drained and rinsed • 425g (15oz) can chickpeas, drained and rinsed • 2 shallots, finely chopped • **For the vinaigrette:** 30ml (2 tbsp) lemon juice • salt and freshly ground black pepper • 2 tsp runny honey • 125ml (4fl oz) extra-virgin olive oil • 3 tbsp chopped fresh mint • 4 tbsp roughly chopped flat-leaf parsley • mint sprigs and grated lemon rind, to garnish

What to do

1. Put the drained beans and chickpeas and the shallots in a serving bowl.
2. To make the vinaigrette, whisk together the lemon juice, seasoning and honey. Gradually whisk in the oil and stir in the chopped herbs.
3. Spoon the dressing over the bean mixture, mix well, then garnish and serve.

Vegetable and Chickpea Couscous

Today's quick-cook varieties of couscous simply require soaking in boiling water to achieve a fluffy, soft grain.

Preparation time: 15 minutes • Cooking time: 20 minutes • 284 calories per serving • Serves 6

What you need

350g (12oz) each onions, carrots and fennel, cut into large chunks • 1.1 litres (2 pints) vegetable stock • 2 bay leaves • salt and freshly ground black pepper • 350g (12oz) courgettes, cut into large chunks • 1 large red pepper, deseeded and cut into large chunks • 400g (14oz) can chickpeas, drained and rinsed • 350g (12oz) couscous • 25g (1oz) butter

What to do

1. Put the onions, carrots and fennel in a large saucepan with the vegetable stock and bay leaves and season well. Bring slowly to the boil and cook for 5–10 minutes, or until the vegetables begin to soften.

2. Remove from the heat, add the courgettes, red pepper and chickpeas, return to the boil and cook for 3–4 minutes.

3. Meanwhile, soak the couscous, according to the packet instructions, with 1 tsp salt. Melt the butter in a large, deep frying pan. Add the couscous, breaking up the grains with a fork, heat through and season.

4. Add the hot vegetables to the couscous and serve.

Mixed Mushroom Risotto

Dal with Red Pepper

Pasta with Creamy Pesto Sauce

This is a creamy and surprisingly low-fat version of the classic Italian sauce. It will keep for up to a week if kept in an air-tight jar in the refrigerator.

Preparation time: 8 minutes • Cooking time: 5 minutes • 538 calories per serving • Serves 4

What you need

5 tbsp freshly grated Parmesan cheese • 25g (1oz) pine nuts, toasted • 200g (7oz) tub low-fat fromage frais • 2 garlic cloves • 40g (1½ oz) fresh basil leaves, torn • 40g (1½ oz) fresh parsley, roughly chopped • salt and freshly ground black pepper • 450g (1lb) fresh tagliatelle

What to do

1. Put the Parmesan, pine nuts, fromage frais and garlic cloves in a food processor and whizz to a thick paste. Add the herbs and whizz for a further 2–3 seconds. Scrape the mixture into a bowl and season generously.
2. Cook the pasta in a large saucepan of boiling salted water, according to the packet instructions. Drain thoroughly, stir in the pesto sauce and adjust the seasoning to taste.

Herb, Lemon and Crispy Crumb Pasta

A traditional Sicilian recipe that makes a perfect light summer dish served with a green salad.

Preparation time: 10 minutes • Cooking time: 10 minutes • 567 calories per serving • Serves 4

What you need

3 tbsp chopped flat-leaf parsley • 8 tbsp chopped fresh basil • grated rind of 1 lemon, plus 30ml (2 tbsp) juice • 200ml (7fl oz) tub crème fraîche • salt and freshly ground black pepper • 15ml (1 tbsp) olive oil • 4 tbsp fresh breadcrumbs • 350g (12oz) pasta, such as fusilli

What to do

1. Mix together the herbs, lemon rind and juice and the crème fraîche in a large bowl, then season well.

2. Heat the olive oil in a frying pan and fry the breadcrumbs for 5 minutes, or until golden brown. Drain on kitchen paper and set aside.

3. Meanwhile, cook the pasta in a large saucepan of boiling salted water, according to the packet instructions. Drain well, return the pasta to the pan, stir in the crème fraîche mixture and heat through. Sprinkle the fried breadcrumbs over the pasta and serve immediately.

Dal with Red Pepper

This spicy lentil dish is created from convenient store cupboard ingredients, which can now be easily found in organic sections in shops.

Preparation time: 20 minutes • Cooking time: 15 minutes • 395 calories per serving for 4; 263 calories per serving for 6 • Serves 4–6

What you need

425g (15oz) can chickpeas, drained and rinsed • 2 x 300g (11oz) cans green lentils, drained and rinsed • squeeze of lemon juice • 45ml (3 tbsp) corn oil or ghee • 1 tsp cumin seeds • 1 tsp ground coriander • 1 large onion, finely chopped • 1 large red pepper, deseeded and chopped • 1 tsp chopped fresh root ginger • 2 large garlic cloves, crushed • 1 large green chilli, deseeded and finely chopped • freshly ground black pepper • 1 tsp salt

What to do

1. Sprinkle the chickpeas and lentils with the lemon juice and set aside.

2. Put the oil and spices in a heavy-based pan and cook over a medium heat until the cumin seeds start to pop. Add the onion, pepper, ginger, garlic and chilli, and cook until the onions are translucent. Remove from the heat.

3. In a separate pan, combine the chickpeas and lentils with 45–60ml (3–4 tbsp) water and bring to the boil. Reduce the heat to a simmer, cover and cook for 10 minutes. Drain off any excess moisture and lightly mash the chickpeas and lentils.

4. Add the pepper mixture, stir well. Season and serve.

family matters

As a parent you will find yourself on the receiving end of a constant stream of advice – from friends, relatives, experts and other parents. For what everyone wants is the best for their children and to be able to provide a happy and secure and, above all, a healthy environment for their family. Turning organic is therefore an obvious choice for parents, providing not only the best of products for their family's health and well-being, but also contributing towards improving the environment and wildlife and therefore creating a brighter future for everyone's children.

conception and pregnancy

Starting a family and becoming a parent is, as anyone who has experienced it knows, a time when perceptions and attitudes change and priorities alter. Above all else, we want to be able to give our baby the best possible start in life.

Organics and conception

A healthy diet is believed to affect male and female fertility and therefore conception. Getting the right balance of vitamins and minerals and particularly including organic food in our diet could be vital, and should also reduce the likelihood of developing problems during pregnancy and birth. After all, if both mum and dad are healthy and fit when they conceive, there is every chance that baby will be, too.

Planning an organic baby

Make a list of all the things you could do to improve your lifestyle and maximize your health and fitness. The sooner you do it, the better.

● Go organic now – organic foods are free from GM foods. They are also free from chemical additives, which may be harmful to the developing foetus

● Grow your own – by growing your own fruit and vegetables you will know exactly the origins of what you are eating

● Find out about organic suppliers – look into organic box schemes and mail-order services offering a home delivery service of organically grown produce

● Drink lots of water – water helps the body to absorb vital minerals and vitamins.

There are fears that tap water may contain some toxic residues so use a water filter and buy bottled water when travelling

● Take supplements if needed – zinc, selenium and folic acid are all recommended for preconception and during pregnancy to help limit birth defects such as spina bifida, other neural tube defects and many others

● Find an alternative health practitioner – consult a health practitioner for the supplements that will be right for you. Consult a homeopath or naturopath to find out what measures you should take

● Get fit – enrol on an exercise programme that suits you

● Learn relaxation techniques – yoga and stretching, Pilates, aromatherapy and many other forms of relaxation can help sustain a healthy pregnancy and birth

● Look to your lifestyle and avoid exposure to everyday toxic chemicals as far as possible – buy environmentally friendly cleaning products and decorate baby's room with organic paints

● Read as much as you can, so you can make informed choices

Avoid:

● Non-organic food and drinks

● Over-processed and refined foods

● Caffeine and alcohol, which can inhibit the absorption of vital nutrients

● Taking antibiotics

● Watch out for harmful substances in everyday products such as hair dyes and shampoos, cleaning agents, cosmetics and skincare creams and lotions

● Don't use fertilizers or sprays

Couples planning a pregnancy or those who have had problems conceiving can consult organizations concerned with preconceptual care (*see Organic Directory*). These offer nutritional and lifestyle advice, believing that in maximizing the health of the parents (and therefore by inference the ova and sperm), it is possible to reduce, and in most cases eliminate, infertility and other problems associated with conception and birth.

One preconception programme recommended to couples involves them eating an organic diet for at least three or four months before conception, preferably longer. A recent British research study involved 367 couples who had previously had problems conceiving: they had an 80 per cent success rate using this method. It is also thought that if couples can work at the nutritional side and deficiencies before they go for IVF the success rate rises from 15 to 50 per cent.

The widespread use of chemicals in modern farming methods and the potential threats to male fertility from the use of pesticides are currently of major concern. It appears that men who eat organic food have higher sperm counts, and women with moderately low body fat who eat a healthy organic diet seem likely to have the best chance of conception and healthy pregnancy – because less fat means a reduction in levels of potential toxins that may be stored in fat.

Although the medical profession and scientific community are still sceptical about the role of diet and fertility and preconceptual care, many experts agree that eating a healthy, well-balanced diet can have an impact. If you ensure you eat a nutritious and healthy balanced diet, you are most likely to have an easier conception and a healthy pregnancy.

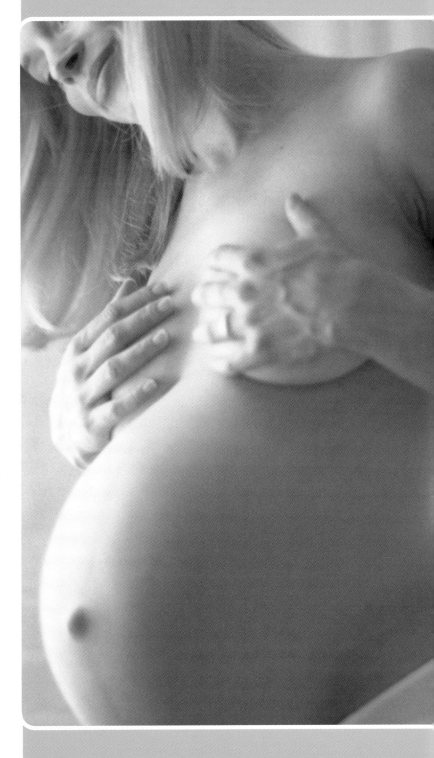

You're pregnant!

The first few weeks of pregnancy is a time of extremely rapid growth and development for the baby. The spinal cord, heart and all the vital organs are forming and by the end of eight weeks the baby will have quadrupled in size. As baby grows, she will need more and more nourishment. A healthy diet is paramount as the nutrients from everything that you eat will pass through to the baby.

A healthy diet

There are certainly fewer pesticides and synthetic chemicals in organic foods than in non-organically farmed foods, but little data currently exists comparing the nutritional benefits of organic and non-organic foods. Evidence suggests that organic foods can contain more trace vitamins and minerals than non-organic, particularly vitamins A and C, more protein and increased concentrations of zinc and iron. Eating an organic diet is also all about taking care of what you eat, so this awareness can only be good for your health and therefore for a developing baby.

Healthy guidelines

It is vital to eat plenty of protein during pregnancy. Protein provides essential amino acids for building new tissues and a healthy immune system. Buy organic meat, fish, poultry, dairy products and eggs. If organic fish is unavailable try and buy wild fish rather than farmed.

Carbohydrates are a major source of stored energy. Buy organic potatoes, lentils, beans and peas as well as oats, grains and brown rice, which also provide fibre, vitamins and minerals. Fats are also a prime source of energy, both saturated and unsaturated. Unsaturated fats include mono- and polyunsaturated fats. Omega-3, the polyunsaturated fats found in oil-rich fish such as sardines, salmon and mackerel, and in soya beans and rapeseed oil, are necessary for brain development in the foetus.

Preparing for the birth

A healthy lifestyle during pregnancy helps ensure that the experience of birth will be as stress- and problem-free as possible. Also help yourself by being well prepared.

- Decide what intervention is acceptable in advance, and ask your doctor or homeopath for details of the homeopathic birthing kit
- Make a list of all the things you may need in hospital or for the first few days after baby's birth, and have them to hand
- If you'll be spending time in hospital take a few organic snacks such as fresh fruit and organic cereal bars to give you energy, and take plenty of bottled water

Vitamins and minerals

An organic, healthy and well-balanced diet should provide you with the nutrients needed for a healthy pregnancy, but vitamin and mineral supplements may be helpful. Calcium is vital to build healthy bones and teeth and for muscles. Your baby's bones begin to form between weeks four and six after conception, so it is vital that calcium is high prior to conception and is kept at optimum levels during pregnancy. Eat plenty of dairy products, leafy green vegetables and soya. Vitamin D helps calcium absorption, so include organic eggs and cheese. B-complex vitamins are needed for the healthy formation of red blood cells, for a healthy nervous system and for converting food into energy. Find them in yeast, eggs, organic soya beans, mackerel, sardines, wheatgerm, avocados, nuts and sunflower seeds.

Iron is necessary to make haemoglobin, which carries oxygen in the blood to your baby. While pregnant, you may need to increase your iron intake by up to 100 per cent. Iron is found in lean meat, sardines, egg yolks, fortified breakfast cereals, green leafy vegetables and parsley. Antioxidant vitamin C helps in the absorption of iron, and is essential for the formation of healthy gums, teeth, bones and skin. Find it in citrus fruit, strawberries, kiwi fruit, tomatoes, peppers, broccoli and tomatoes. Folic acid is vital to the growth of new cells before conception and during pregnancy; it can be found in dark green leafy vegetables, pulses, nuts seeds, cereals and bread.

Zinc is found in seafood, red meat and sunflower seeds. It is vital for many hormonal activities, for normal brain development, and to ensure the healthy development of the baby's immune system. An inorganic diet is often deficient in zinc because chemical fertilizers can inhibit plants from absorbing this vital mineral from the soil. The level of selenium also depends greatly on the soil, with food processing further depleting this mineral from our diet. Selenium is essential for normal sexual development and deficiency can result in impaired reproductive performance. Organically grown and reared meat and dairy products, fish, citrus fruit, brazil nuts, avocados and lentils are likely to contain the most selenium due to healthy soil practices.

the organic baby

The 'organic' label extends way beyond just food. And just as diet is an important part of ensuring a healthy happy baby, creating an ecologically sound environment in which your baby can develop should be of equal concern. Preparation is the key to enjoying those first important months in a baby's life.

Get ready

One area where you can plan and prepare for the big arrival is in the nursery. There are many alarming concerns about the safety of some plastics, textiles, soft furnishings, paints, bedding and clothing. Use common sense, budget wisely to accommodate baby's needs, and shop around to find the best-quality products at sensible prices.

Natural fabrics

Try to find the most natural fabrics, organically grown if possible, with which to decorate baby's nursery. Non-organically grown cotton is one of the most widely sprayed crops and research has found that these insecticides and other residues can remain in the cloth for some time. Other materials are treated with flame-retardant chemicals, which have been associated with cot death.

Unbleached and undyed fabrics are widely available and there are many mail-order companies, which offer a convenient and affordable way to buy these very aesthetically pleasing goods. You will be pleasantly surprised to find that choice isn't limited to cottons and hemps. Organic denims, silks, wools, flannel and linen are all available, in a range of colours. There is also a boom in the number of baby shops opening that stock a large selection of 'green baby' goods such as organic cotton and woollen clothing, blankets, bedding and other everyday baby necessities.

Natural colour

Although all the natural fabrics and furnishings help create a calm and soothing atmosphere for the home and nursery, you can create a splash of colour with items coloured with plant or mineral-extract natural dyes. A good range of natural organic paints and natural mineral pigments are available in a wide palette of colours (*see Chapter 5*). The colours are often rather muted and suit a nursery.

Consider natural floor coverings as an alternative to carpet. Wood is easy to maintain, can be wiped clean and can be scattered with natural wool rugs for warmth. There is also a great selection of natural carpets, which have become understandably fashionable. Coir, jute and seagrass carpets are widely available from many carpet shops and home-furnishing department stores as well as other shops catering for the environmentally friendly consumer. When planning the nursery remember that babies spend a great deal of their lives sleeping (although many new mothers may argue with this), so creating a natural, chemical-free sleeping space is high on the list of priorities. An increasing number of companies now sell organic bedding – mattresses, pillowcases, sheets, duvets and duvet covers and blankets are all available from many mail-order companies, via the Internet and from some of the new 'green baby' shops.

You may not have the budget to create a totally organic nursery, so make your choices based on priorities. For example, what does baby need most, where will she be spending most of her time, what can you afford now and what will be needed initially? If an organic mattress is not an option, look into alternatives such as untreated cottons; the same goes for clothing and fabrics. A very popular baby product of recent years has been sheepskin – used for baby to lie on, both at home and when out and about. Sheepskin keeps baby cool in summer and warm in winter. You can find untreated and organic sheepskins.

You will probably find you are inundated with gifts of baby-wear with the arrival of the baby, but it is also wise to invest in a few special things beforehand. Many mail-order companies will deliver within two weeks, but it is worth buying well in advance so that you are prepared. Especially for the newborn, it is worth investing in organic cotton and wool clothing, wonderfully soft for baby's sensitive skin. You will probably need at least three little romper suits and the same amount of all-in-one vests, an over-cardigan and little hat. As with any other products, always read the labels carefully and buy from reputable shops and outlets, as 'natural' on a product does not always mean chemical-free!

Eco-nappies

Over nine million disposable nappies are used in Britain every day and now make up over 4 per cent of British household waste – that's about 800,000 tonnes of nappy waste a year. Used nappies cause tremendous environmental damage as they take up landfill sites and can take several years to rot down and leach their chemicals into the land and waterways. Nappies also cause pollution in their manufacture and over seven million trees a year are felled in the production of disposables.

There has also been recent concern raised about the chemical wetting agent applied to disposables to help keep the baby's bottom drier. Reusable nappies certainly seem the best choice. According to a recent study by the Women's Environmental Network you could save up to £600 an infant by using washables, while helping to reduce the total national cost of using disposables – the cost of disposing of them currently stands at £40 million per year. Choosing organic reusable nappies is a positive step for the health of your baby and the planet. If you lead a very busy life you could join one of the increasing number of nappy-washing services, which collect soiled nappies and deliver freshly laundered ones in return.

Sometimes you may need to use disposable nappies. In this case, choose the environmentally friendly versions that are now appearing on chemist and supermarket shelves.

Best for babies' bottoms

Avoid using baby wipes. They can inhibit baby's natural oils from doing their job and they contain chemicals, such as preservatives, alcohol and perfume. It is just as simple to use organic cotton wool or a reusable cotton muslin and water. Add a few drops of lavender essential oil to the water if preferred. You can always carry a small container of water when travelling and a pack of cotton wool. Nappy creams are also unnecessary. A natural cream such as calendula or camomile cream can act as a barrier or can clear nappy rash. A few drops of lavender oil diluted in water is also a good cure for nappy rash. The other creams are very strong for a young baby's sensitive skin.

Skincare

Pregnant women and small babies are especially targeted by marketing companies trying to encourage sales of the many bodycare creams, lotions and other toiletries. These are also the most sensitive group to the perfumes, additives and chemicals used in these goods. Fortunately, there are now many organic and natural alternatives for mother and baby – from moisturizers to nappy creams, cleansers, shampoos and soaps. Many companies offer a range of goods made with organic ingredients, which are good for the skin and kind to the environment. It is worth shopping around to find the best range to suit you and baby, and remember that many toiletries are non-essentials, especially in baby's first year when the body's natural oils should be left to do their own work.

A healthy organic diet

Babies and children are more at risk from any chemical residues found in non-organic foods than adults because of their high food intake compared with their body weight. Babies are especially vulnerable to toxins from pesticides, man-made chemicals and additives because of their rapid development and growth. While their organs are developing and their immune systems are immature they are additionally unable to excrete potentially harmful toxins.

Breastfeeding

'Breast is best' is the message promoted by many campaigners, for example the World Health Organization (WHO), the World Wildlife Fund (WWF), the National Childbirth Trust (NCT), the Women's Environmental Network (WEN) and other organizations set up to help new mothers. Breastfeeding helps to establish that special bond between mother and baby, providing comfort and security. Breast milk is also the most nutritious fast food. It contains all the nutrients a baby needs for the first six months of its life; to help him or her fight infections and build up immunity, to promote intelligence and to improve development of the nervous system.

Even the quality of breast milk and the many benefits of breastfeeding have come under close scrutiny recently. Among the many food scares in the past decade, one of the most worrying has been the threat of potential contaminants found in breast milk due to poor maternal health and environmental pollution. But the benefits of breastfeeding are enormous,and if you lead an organic lifestyle any potential risks are greatly reduced.

The Benefits of Breastfeeding

The best way to feed your baby is the way that feels right for you – although it it clear to see that breastfeeding has many advantages for babies – as well as for you.

● food always on tap, ready to serve at right temperature. no preparation necessary, such as sterilising and heating. economical.

● no damage to environment, from packaging, sterilising, cleaning, transportation etc.

● suckling creates bond between mother and baby. increases resistance to infection and builds immunity against diseases

● is said to help prevent breast cancer and ovarian cancer in women if they breastfeed.

● is said to increase motor development skills and nervous system development in children

● associated with reduced risk of Sudden Infant Death reduced risk of gastric and respiratory infections and excema and diabetes.

Organic baby milks

Not every mother is able to feed her baby herself, and for those mums who are unable to breastfeed, or who have decided to discontinue breastfeeding, a number of organic formula milks are available from healthfood shops, mail-order companies and supermarkets.

A healthy start

When your baby is about five to six months old, solids should be introduced into her diet to provide extra nourishment for her accelerated growth. Weaning, for a new parent, is often a time of great angst, but by following a simple sequence of introducing one food at a time, starting with those foods that are most easily digested, weaning can be a time of excitement as your baby begins the journey of discovering and enjoying good food. Early foods must be puréed or mashed, with no lumps. Introduce one food at a time so if there is any allergic reaction you will know what caused it. After a few weeks you will be able to start combining foods. There is a great selection of organic foods available, but try and choose those that are locally produced and in season.

Baby food market

The organic baby food market is booming, with one in three babies now eating organic, so there is a huge range of organic baby foods to choose from. There are also plenty of organic juices and drinks, but try and keep these to a minimum, giving your baby water to quench thirst rather than sweet juices, which are not good for their teeth.

Make-your-own versus ready-made

Although bought baby foods are convenient and easy to use, especially when going out for the day or busy with the demands a new baby brings, they really should be used as one-offs, rather than become part of the everyday repertoire. Try and make your own as much as possible. This has distinct advantages: you know exactly what goes into each and every meal and how fresh it is; it is also much cheaper. The vast range of organic foods now available from pastas, fruit, vegetables, rice, grains and lentils, means you can make the diet as varied as you like. By making your own foods you will also be helping to save the environment too as packaging is the ultimate cost of buying ready-made baby foods.

Preparing and storing a simple purée

Sometimes it is convenient to prepare baby foods in advance. A particularly ideal way is to freeze small quantities of freshly prepared organic fruit and vegetable purées.

- Steam or lightly boil one vegetable such as carrot or potato, or a selection of vegetables or fruit such as carrots, parsnips and apple if you have started combining foods
- Drain well then mix with boiled water, breast or formula milk and purée to the desired consistency
- Leave to cool, then freeze in ice-cube trays
- When frozen, transfer to freezer bags or a container, label clearly and date
- Reheat thoroughly when ready to serve and cool before serving to baby

Introducing solids

Follow these basic guidelines to gradually wean your baby on to solids – introducing one new food at a time and progressively adding new textures and combinations.

3–6 months
Serve as purée, with no lumps.

sweet potatoes, carrots, parsnips, swede, most root vegetables; broccoli, courgettes, apples, banana, pears, baby rice, potato flour, millet

6–9 months
Serve slightly thicker textures, but avoid big lumps.

potatoes, peas, beans, avocado, peaches, apricots, melon, plums, herbs, vegetable oils, linseed and olive oil

9–12 months
Baby should be learning to chew now. Introduce finger foods.

dairy products: yogurt, milk, butter, egg yolk, tomatoes, sweet pepper, wheat (but be careful), pasta, rice, breadsticks, meat, fish, oranges and other citrus fruits, most soft fruits, dried fruits

12 months up
Baby will be willing to try new foods and tastes so introduce stronger flavours and different textures.

cheese, egg white, lentils, other beans and pulses, honey, wheat, berry fruits, such as strawberries, blackberries etc., kiwis

Over two
Nuts should not be given to children under five years old.

shellfish

organic toddler

By the time your baby becomes a toddler – from about fifteen months on – many of his or her eating habits will already have been formed. The most important thing, apart from eating a healthy diet, is to encourage mealtimes to be fun, not a chore. This is important so that your child will always have a healthy respect and enjoyment for food, and so that you can enjoy family mealtimes, where children will learn good eating habits and discover that eating can be a time for fun and togetherness. If it is impossible to buy everything organic, due to cost or availability, try to make the mainstay foods of your toddler's diet organic.

Nutrition and growing needs

By the time a child is two years old she will be able to eat virtually the same meals as you are preparing for yourself. She should have several teeth and have learnt chewing skills and be feeding herself, with a little help. Encourage this as your child will enjoy this new-found independence and will love being praised for what she can achieve, even if there is a lot of mess. This is also the time when a toddler's tastebuds are developing, and by introducing more tasty and even spicy foods and foods with stronger flavours and a variety of textures you will encourage more adventurous eating habits in the future.

Toddlers are often very active so it is often better to have a routine of eating four or five smaller meals a day rather than three large ones. This is firstly, because your toddler will not want to sit and concentrate on eating for very long and, secondly, because throughout the day she will need refuelling as she burns off that seemingly boundless energy that toddlers have. A mid-morning and a mid-afternoon snack is often very welcome and this is where you can encourage your toddler to enjoy healthy organic snacks to keep them going.

Balancing act

Toddlers will benefit from eating at least two portions of organic fish a week to supply them with the all-important omega-3 oils needed for brain development and a healthy nervous system. Organic lean red meat is an excellent source of iron, needed for energy and red blood cell formation, as are egg yolks, oatmeal, bananas, brown rice, potatoes, green peas, prunes, sunflower seeds and green leafy vegetables.

Calcium is needed for healthy bones and teeth. Search for organic cheese, milk, green leafy vegetables, tofu, almonds, soya beans and dried beans with which to feed your child.

Minerals are needed just as much as vitamins. The amount of minerals in the food we eat depends very largely on the levels of minerals in the soil where the food is grown. This is why it is argued that organic foods are more nutritious, because the soil in which they are grown is often healthy and full of nutrients.

Making your own foods rather than opting for the ready-made organic foods will obviously cut the cost of your shopping. You can involve your toddler in the preparing and making of favourite foods, which will serve to fuel their interest and tempt them further to eat well and enjoy the fruits of their labours.

Supplements

You may feel the need to give your toddler supplements. Many people believe it is essential so that growth and development remain at optimum levels, especially at times of illness or when your child is going through a phase of not eating much. Pollution from the environment can affect our absorption of vitamins and minerals and especially those of the young and developing child. However, supplements should be treated as just that, to be used alongside a healthy and well-balanced diet. You should consult your doctor or a nutritionist before you decide which supplement to give your child. It is very important to give children the correct doses as they are more sensitive than adults to overdoses of vitamins and minerals. Try to choose those supplements that are of a high quality without any added 'nasties'. Healthfood shops are usually very helpful in recommending good brands.

Snack organic

Encourage your children to learn healthy eating habits from an early age by giving them healthy snacks of organic foods.

FRESH FRUITS

Fresh fruits are an excellent snack. Non-organic fruits have been found to have a high amount of pesticide residues

Recipe ideas

Fresh fruits can be mixed into fruit salads, cooked to purées, added to crumbles and jellies or simply enjoyed straight from the fruit bowl. Use organic fruits to make smoothies with natural organic yogurts or milkshakes with organic milk; these will fill your toddler up and provide a slow release of energy. You can try juicing as well, but always dilute pure juice by one part juice to five parts water

Nutritional value

Most fruits are high in vitamin C and are a good source of dietary fibre; bananas provide B-vitamins and potassium

DRIED FRUITS

Dried fruits, too can become a firm favourite and make a great alternative to some of the sweet sugary snacks. They are sweet and chewy and provide an excellent snack food for when you are out and about. Try to choose organic, unsulfurated dried fruits with nothing added other than the fruits' own concentrated sugars and goodness

Recipe ideas

Boil dried fruits in a syrup of water and apple juice, then simmer until softened, to make a fruit compôte. Add dried fruits to breads, breakfast cereals and fresh fruit salads

Nutritional value

Good source of iron and vitamin C

RAW VEGETABLES AND SALADS

Fresh salads and crunchy raw vegetables provide a great, healthy snack.

Recipe ideas

Cut vegetables into little batons and serve with a dip or make little sandwiches and salads with a tasty dressing

Nutritional value

Organic vegetables can provide beta-carotene, potassium and many other important minerals and vitamins for the growing toddler

BREADSTICKS, RICE CAKES AND PLAIN BISCUITS

A handy snack to take with you when you are out and about.

Recipe ideas

Dip into fruit purées or yogurts, savoury dips and soups

Nutritional value

A good source of calcium and iron

Eco-toddler

As well as a healthy diet, you can take many positive steps throughout the home to create a healthy ambience and organic home (*see Chapter 5*) for your children. Start with the toys that they play with. It is extremely tempting to 'treat' your children to a new little plaything every so often, and before you know it your house has become a jungle of plastic, colourful toys. There are toys with batteries that constantly run out and need replacing, toys that are one-minute wonders and others that are played and played with, until they are simply worn out. It's worth thinking about the whole issue of toys when buying. What happens to the old or broken toys? Do they simply get piled on top of the already overflowing rubbish heap? If they're plastic, what hope do we have of them ever rotting down? Can they be recycled, passed on? Are they lasting, or are they bound to be discarded within a few weeks or months?

Positive steps to healthy play

Try to buy second-hand toys, books and games whenever possible. Many parents seem to build up a network of passing on toys to younger children in the family and to friends within their community. Always wash and clean them thoroughly and watch out for broken or unsafe toys. Similarly, do pass your childrens' toys on to family and friends when they have outgrown them.

Try to buy wooden toys, many of which are made from wood from sustainable resources. Ensure that non-toxic paints are used, too. There are some wonderful toys made from untreated organic fabrics or recycled materials and natural rubber. Such dolls, doll's houses, cuddly toys, jigsaws and educational games are all widely available from the many mail-order companies and natural toy shops. When you buy soft toys be aware of the fillings and choose those stuffed with wool, cotton and other natural fibres. Although a little more effort is involved in sourcing the best and healthiest toys possible, it can often mean you receive even more pleasure with the end result.

Avoid toys made from PVC. Recent research on the health effects of phthalates in PVC toys has identified a wide range of chronic affects caused by PVC. When sucked or chewed, PVC can be potentially hazardous to children. PVC is also an environmental danger, both in its manufacture and its disposal.

children's
eating habits

By setting a good example early on, the chances are that your children will establish healthy eating habits. However, there are always problems and challenges to face throughout the childhood years as regards eating patterns: peer pressure, questions over whether school dinners are a better alternative to packed lunches, faddy eating and the craving for junk food inspired by advertising and marketing. But by starting the way you mean to go on, children soon learn what is and isn't allowed.

family matters

Feeding for the future

As children grow their dietary needs change. More protein and calories are needed to sustain the healthy growth of strong bones and teeth, a healthy nervous system and to maintain a healthy immune system. Always ensure that your child drinks enough water. Water helps the body to omit toxins and keeps the body flushed out.

Until the age of five, children should drink about 600ml (1 pint) of milk a day, or an alternative if the child is allergic to dairy produce. Organic milk is readily available and full-fat whole milk should always be given to children in preference to skimmed or semi-skimmed milk. Similarly, organic whole-fat yogurts and cheese are also better – the high fat content is important because of the high energy needs of children.

Always include plenty of fruit and vegetables in your child's diet. The recommendation is five portions of fruit and vegetables a day. However, children do have problems

digesting large amounts of high-fibre foods, and a high-fibre diet can interfere with a child's absorption of iron and calcium. Peanuts should not be given to children before the age of seven to avoid any allergy problems later in life.

Packed lunches versus school dinners

Packed lunches are usually needed for nursery school-age children. A good balanced lunch could be made up with some fresh fruit or vegetables for vitamins, organic whole-meal bread sandwiches or pasta salad for carbohydrates, with cheese, meat or fish for protein and some fat such as a yogurt for energy, with some dried fruit for an energy snack. Keep varying the lunch box to avoid your child getting bored with their food.

School dinners are often a good choice for busy mums. However these are unlikely to be made from organic foods. You could talk to the school about how the catering is organized. It is often the case that catering companies now in charge of school dinners are avoiding GM foods, but you may want to make sure. Some schools have changed to an organic diet. It is certainly possible, so you may be able to drum up the support of other parents and teachers to make it a feasible alternative.

Junk food dilemma

When children start school the peer pressure to conform is enormous and parents often find that children start demanding more 'junk foods' – burgers, chips, pizza, ice creams, chocolates and sweets. The good news is that there is a solution to feeding this craving. You can make healthy fast foods by using natural flavours and organic foods. You can make burgers from organic minced meats. Organic white bread is a healthy alternative. You can buy organic pizza bases. Chips can be a good source of Vitamin C but do limit the number of times each week that chips are offered to avoid too much deep-fried food in your children's diet.

Organic ice cream is a real treat. Made with organic milk, cream, sugar and pure fruits it contains very few added ingredients and no artificial additives or flavourings. Organic yogurts also contain only real ingredients – fruit, cream, milk and no artificial additives or flavourings, and they often contain less sugar and no refined white sugar. Plain yogurts mixed with fresh fruit or a little honey are an attractive dessert for children and there are organic frozen yogurt desserts, too.

Many of the non-organic junk foods such as crisps, sweets, drinks, cereals and yogurts are highly advertised. The organic healthier choices are not, which means we are not paying the price of all the marketing, so prices are fairly competitive. If you completely ban sweets and the other foods that children are automatically attracted to, you will only serve to feed that craving for the forbidden fruits. It is better instead to allow your child a few sweet and other 'treats' in limited quantities, and make these as healthy a choice as possible.

childhood health

By leading an organic lifestyle, you and your family should enjoy good health, but children are inevitably exposed to many common childhood diseases, colds and coughs; and babies often suffer from common ailments associated with teething and colic. There are many alternative therapies available (*see Chapter 4*). Consult naturopaths and homeopaths and look into alternative remedies such as Bach flower remedies, aromatherapy and herbal remedies and even acupuncture and cranial osteopathy.

Teething

Babies can suffer anything from sore and painful gums, ear infections, vomiting, diarrhoea, burning cheeks and nappy rash when teething. Camomile calms a teething baby and can ease the pain associated with teething. You can also buy teething granules, which ease pain and help ease diarrhoea and burning cheeks.

Nappy rash

Teething can often cause excess acid, which in turn may cause nappy rash from the stools or diarrhoea. This can be treated with camomile or calendula cream. Change baby's nappy regularly. Diet may cause nappy rash; if the stools are not normal, avoid acidic foods and make a note of any possible food intolerance. Leave baby's bottom to air whenever possible.

Colic

As any parent knows, colic in a new baby, often occurring between the ages of two and six months, can be the source of the greatest stress. Colic can be caused by food intolerance, either from the mother's breast milk or from formula milk if a baby has a lactose intolerance, or from trapped wind. Looking at your own diet if breastfeeding, or your baby's diet if baby is on formula milk or has moved on to solids can alleviate the problem greatly. You can try herbs such as fennel, dill, camomile, or ginger infused in boiling water, then cooled. You can also buy infant bacteria, which can be added to baby's feed or water, to help balance the levels of healthy bacteria in the gut. A cranial osteopath can often sort out many childhood illnesses, such as colic, vomiting or sleep problems, and can even help prevent problems in later life, such as a bad back, in just a few visits.

Coughs and colds

Especially in the winter months you may find your child is constantly sniffly and suffering from a cough or cold. Homeopaths can recommend a suitable remedy to suit your child. You may also look at diet: dairy products, wheat and grains can often cause the build-up of toxins that result in mucus in your child's nasal passages. Give your child more liquids, especially water, to help them cleanse themselves of these toxins. There are a number of herbal cough and cold remedies, but always consult a qualified practitioner for advice, especially with young children.

Eczema and asthma

Many babies suffer from eczema, which can be related to food intolerance. It is worth looking at diet above all to help cure this preventable condition. An organic diet can help eliminate many problems related to eczema and asthma as the food is so unadulterated. For eczema, try applying pure evening primrose oil or vitamin E oil directly to the skin. Evening primrose oil and fish oils taken orally can also help. Zinc (in sunflower seeds and red meat) and vitamin A (in liver, milk, butter, cheese, egg yolks and oil-rich fish) are also helpful. Always consult your practitioner, homeopath or naturopath.

Bumps and bangs

Apply arnica cream to a bruise, or arnica tablets to relieve any shock and pain from the bumps and bangs. Calendula cream is good for cuts and grazes.

Immunizations

This is an area of great contention and one that is a very personal choice for parents. It is impossible to cover all the pros and cons here as the issue of immunization is such a minefield and an area that is constantly being debated as new research comes to light. The most important thing to remember is that you do have a choice. Read as much as you can to understand all the arguments for and against. Naturopaths, homeopaths and your GP and health visitor can all give you helpful advice.

as nature
intended

Since a healthy body comes from within, this chapter looks at how to feel good and have a glowing skin by eating a balanced diet and taking care of your body. Your skin and hair need loving attention and chemical-free beauty products with ingredients such as jojoba and rose provide essential natural goodness – you can even try making your own beauty products. To build on the effects of a chemical-free diet, take regular exercise to tone the muscles, keep in shape and give your vital body organs a good workout. If illness does strike there are choices available to you other than conventional medicine. Keep an alternative medicine chest with simple remedies such as homeopathic and herbal treatments, or try complementary therapies such as osteopathy and acupuncture, which can cure a wide range of ailments.

a healthy lifestyle

To look and feel good you need to take care of your body's needs. By eating a balanced, nutritious diet rich in organic foods you will take in good levels of vitamins and minerals – essential for cell growth and efficient body functioning. There is no point eating a healthy organic diet if you don't also look after the functioning and health of your body, so take regular exercise to tone the muscles and keep in shape.

Eating for good health

In the stress-filled lives that many of us lead today, a good diet often gets neglected and junk and processed food is consumed instead. This can lead to us feeling run down, and being susceptible to illness. For our bodies to work efficiently we need a daily intake of vitamins, minerals, complex carbohydrates, protein, fats and fibre.

Fruit and vegetables contain high levels of vitamins and minerals, particularly the antioxidants, vitamins A, C and E, which fight illness. It is recommended to eat five servings daily (one serving equates to one item of fruit or a portion of vegetables).

Wholemeal bread, wholegrain cereals, pasta, brown rice and potatoes are good sources of complex carbohydrates, which contain B-vitamins, many minerals and fibre. Four to five servings should be eaten daily (one serving equates to one slice of bread or a cup of pasta).

Meat, fish, poultry, nuts, beans and lentils contain good levels of protein, which give the body strength and energy, and two to three servings are needed daily (one serving equates to one portion of meat or fish).

Dairy products such as milk, cheese or yogurt contain fat, and daily intake should be just one or two servings a day (one serving equates to one small carton of yogurt or 500ml/⅞ pint milk). However, they are also high in calcium and phosphorous, which keep bones and teeth healthy.

Fibre swells the food left in the intestine, and then softens it by increasing the water that is retained, helping waste to be easily eliminated. Fibre is contained in wholemeal bread, brown rice, cereals, vegetables and fruits and pulses.

To get the optimum benefit from these foods it is best to eat organically grown crops (see Chapters 1 and 2). Non-organic foods contain more water and have less vitamins and minerals. Organic, chemical-free meat tastes better and has an improved texture; if you love beef, you can be assured it is disease-free.

Taking supplements

Occasionally, in times of extreme stress and when an inadequate diet lacking in fruit and vegetables is being eaten, or if you drink alcohol regularly or smoke, vitamin supplements can become necessary. It can be difficult to work out whether you need B-complex vitamins or perhaps an antioxidant, so try taking a combined vitamin and mineral preparation daily.

Keeping fit

Regular exercise benefits everybody, whatever their age. It can keep your weight even, your skin looking good, and your immune system functioning well. Your heart and lungs receive a good workout, your muscles become toned, and it provides some protection against heart disease. Weight-bearing exercise such as running or tennis can prevent the onset in later life of osteo-porosis (the bone-thinning disease).

When you exercise regularly your body develops suppleness, strength and stamina. Suppleness makes you more flexible and more mobile, exercise tones joints and the supporting ligaments. Strength is the power needed by your muscles to push, lift or move things around. Resistance exercise such as weight-lifting or running up a hill develops muscle strength. Stamina is when you can swim or cycle for longer without becoming out of breath. You also get your body to work aerobically – where your lungs and heart work hard, and breathing and blood circulation increases.

Exercise needs to be enjoyable, so choose a sport or activity you like – it may be working out in the gym, doing an aerobics class, running, playing tennis or just fast walking. To keep fit, it is recommended that you do 30 minutes daily of brisk exercise, if you can't manage this, aim for at least three times a week. If you haven't exercised for a while, start slowly and build up to recommended levels as you get fitter.

complementary
therapies

Concerns have been growing for a while about the increase in allergies and possible links to the polluted atmosphere and the levels of pesticides in our diet. Changing to a more natural, organic diet has therefore become a priority for many. People are also adopting a holistic approach to their bodies, wanting to reach the cause of the disease rather than treating the symptoms. Complementary therapies have therefore become a popular choice in preference to conventional medicine.

The benefits of complementary therapies

Complementary therapies work holistically, often looking at a person's characteristics and emotional reactions to a disease, regarding the symptoms that are manifested as a reaction to an imbalance elsewhere in the system. Treatments such as acupuncture and Chinese herbalism, for example, seek blockages in the body, which are worked on to harmonize the 'energy' levels and bring the body back to balance. There are many different therapies available, some of which are more suitable for certain conditions, but it is worth experimenting to find the therapy for you.

Homeopathy

Homeopathic treatment was used by Hippocrates as early as the fifth century BC, but its ideology was not revived until the late eighteenth century by a German physician called Samuel Hahnemann. Homeopathy's philosophy is to treat 'like' with 'like'. It uses animal, vegetable and mineral preparations to treat a person's illness, seeing the symptoms of a disease as the body's fight to overcome it, so it further stimulates this reaction. A visit to a practitioner will involve you providing him with a detailed case history, answering many questions about yourself and your lifestyle. The prescribed remedy will be personal to you and may be pills, granules or a liquid. Homeopathic treatment does not work for everyone, but can help asthma, irritable bowel syndrome, migraines and skin conditions.

Chinese herbalism

This ancient traditional practice uses different herbs to treat and prevent physical, mental and emotional ill health in people. Diagnosis of a condition is similar to acupuncture (*see below*) and is based on checking the flow of *chi* (energy) in the body and its qualities, *yin* (passive) and *yang* (positive) for any imbalances. There is also the detailed procedure of looking at your face and tongue, touching your body and taking pulses, listening to your voice and breathing, and asking questions about lifestyle and health. The herbal prescription, which can be made into tea, will depend on the severity of your condition. Chinese herbalism can help eczema, depression, hay fever, asthma, migraine and PMS (premenstrual syndrome).

Western herbalism

Our early ancestors long ago recognized that plants could restore the body. Today, herbalism uses the curative powers of plants, flowers, trees and herbs to stimulate the body's innate healing system – the 'vital force'. Here, too, the symptoms of an illness are seen as the body fighting the disease. A therapist will once again take down a long case history, which includes asking about your personality, childhood, eating and sleeping patterns and details of any other illnesses. Herbs will be prescribed to support the body's fight against disease, and to detoxify and boost the immune system. Herbs come in the form of tinctures, creams, compresses, poultices, infusions, decoctions, oils, tablets and capsules.

Aromatherapy

Essential oils were used many years ago by the Greeks and ancient Egyptians, and later in Britain to ward off the plague. But aromatherapy was not fully developed until the 1930s by a French chemist, René-Maurice Gattefossé. Today, around a hundred and fifty essential oils are available. These aromatic essences are mainly extracted by steam distillation from plants, flowers, trees and fruits.

All have healing and therapeutic qualities. The oils can be used in various ways: in aromatherapy massage they are absorbed through the skin via a carrier oil; a few drops can be added to a hot bath; they can be inhaled via diffusers and vaporizers; and some oils can be used neat, for example tea tree and lavender to treat burns or wounds. Consult an aromatherapy practitioner before using undiluted oils on your skin, and if you are pregnant or have a medical condition such as high blood pressure.

Acupuncture

This old Chinese healing therapy is over two thousand years old. Acupuncture works on the same system as Chinese herbalism (*see above*) – that *chi* flows through twelve body meridians, and it is its *yin* and *yang* qualities that need to be balanced for good health. Sterilized needles are inserted in main points along these meridians, which are believed to be connected to the organs, to remove blockages. Again, diagnosis is detailed, the therapist will question you on lifestyle, health and medical history; she will also study your tongue and take your pulses – three on each wrist with up to twenty-eight qualities. Treatment will involve inserting needles into the chosen points. Acupuncture can help arthritis, back pain, stress, depression and gynaecological problems.

Osteopathy

This therapy involves manipulation of the body – skeleton, muscles, ligaments and tissues – to improve joint move-ment and ease muscular pain and to help emotional problems. It was devised in the late nineteenth century by an American doctor, Andrew Taylor Still. An osteopath will want to know when your pain and symptoms first started and what movements and actions affect them. He will take a medical history and ask about previous injuries. He will examine you, noting how your joints move and look for restrictions. Osteopathic treatment can help back problems, tension headaches, sports injuries, arthritis and rheumatism.

Reiki

Reiki, meaning 'universal life force energy', is a holistic hands-on healing technique, which was discovered in the mid-nineteenth century by Dr Mikao Usui in Japan. It is channelled from the universal life force to the client by the healer; the energy goes where it is needed, stimulating the body's own healing mechanism. During the hour-long treatment the healer places her hands on twelve body positions and the energy goes deep into the body where physical illness begins, creating balance by releasing blockages and toxins. It also works on an emotional and mental level.

Reiki helps stress-related problems, colds, viral infections and headaches. It also treats chronic conditions such as ME, asthma and migraine.

Massage

This healing art first became popular with the Greeks and Romans. The treatment has grown out of the human need to touch and to be touched. Massage involves manipulating the body's soft tissues to restore good health. By working on the muscles, ligaments and tendons, the therapist aims to find and remove any muscle knots and tension, soothe the emotions and relieve pain. During a treatment, which normally lasts an hour, the therapist may use a blend of essential oils and different massage techniques to treat your back, body and front, releasing the pain in tight, knotty areas. Massage is effective for stress-related conditions, insomnia, depression, PMT and sciatica. There are many different types of massage, including pressure massage such as shiatsu and reflexology (massage of the feet), remedial massage for sports injuries, aromatherapy massage and manual lymphatic drainage massage to remove toxins.

Reflexology

Also called zone therapy, reflexology works on pressure points and nerve endings on the feet, and sometimes the hands, to stimulate the immune system and the body's own healing system. In a similar way to acupuncture, the points are thought to be linked by 'reflex' zones to muscles and body organs, so that when points are treated all the zone is affected. During the 30–60 minute treatment the reflexologist will massage your feet to relax the joints. He will work with his thumb or finger over each foot, dealing with problem areas, which can feel painful. It is a good preventative therapy and can alleviate stress-linked ailments, eczema, menstrual and digestive problems.

Nutritional therapy

This therapy uses diet to restore the body to health. It is thought that small mineral and vitamin deficiencies can stop the body functioning well. It is a detailed healthcare system relying on three basic diagnoses of the body: food allergies, deficiencies and whether toxic overload exists. A first consultation with a therapist involves her looking at your normal diet and habits, any food intolerances, whether you exercise, your emotional and physical history and any medication details. Sometimes hair or urine is tested for specific deficiencies. With all this information she will compile your special diet, plus any necessary vitamin or mineral supplements. Nutritional therapy particularly helps high blood pressure, tiredness, digestive disorders, post-natal illness and constipation.

alternative healing

For emergency treatment when someone becomes seriously ill or is injured, orthodox medical techniques are essential and necessary, but they can be also be supported by alternative healing remedies. These natural treatments are ideal for building up a useful first-aid kit to treat any minor ailments or upsets, such as cuts, colds or flu that occur in your family at home.

Choosing your remedies

With most complementary therapies, such as homeopathy and herballsm (*see pages 114–117*), the body is viewed holistically so that the treatments prescribed take into account the patient's psychological and emotional profile, making them feel more comfortable as they start to recover. However, when you are building up your alternative medicine cabinet for use at home the remedies you buy inevitably have to be general ones that can give comfort to all the family, and help to relieve pain in digestive upsets or minor accidents and ailments.

The remedies

Many different items can be included in your alternative medicine cabinet but the most useful ones are listed below – you can add other treatments as they are needed. The essential oils are often used in the bath, or some can be applied directly to the skin; over-the-counter homeopathic treatments are generally in tablet form; herbal treatments can sometimes be used in their raw state, as capsules or as teas; Bach flower remedies are available as tinctures.

ESSENTIAL OILS

Lavender

Apply two drops directly to burns and for reducing inflammation. Use diluted for treating headaches and insomnia

Tea tree

A natural antiseptic, several drops can be applied directly to treat cuts and insect bites; good for gargling and throat infections (a drop in a cup of water)

Peppermint

Helps with muscle fatigue (diluted in a carrier oil), stomach upset, morning sickness, travel sickness (couple of drops on a sugar cube) and bad breath (a drop in a cup of water)

Camomile

Soothing and good for insomnia and helping with allergic reactions (use 4–5 drops in a bath)

HOMEOPATHIC REMEDIES

Allium cepa

For violent attacks of hay fever that involve sneezing, streaming eyes and cough

Calendula cream

Can help to relieve the skin irritation of eczema

Arnica

The cream tablets or tincture help reduce the symptoms of shock. Also good for reducing swelling and healing bruises

Aconitum

Take tablets when you first start to sneeze or shiver. Helps runny nose or blocked-up nose in stuffy atmosphere

Gelsemium

For classic flu symptoms with shivering, aching and general tiredness

HERBAL TREATMENTS

Dandelion

Good for alleviating asthma symptoms

Garlic

Useful antiseptic. Can be taken in capsule form to improve functioning of immune system; good for cleansing cholesterol from system, helps prevent colds and will soothe a nagging cough

Ginger

Good for digestion, upset stomach and travel sickness (fresh root can be chewed, made into a tea, or it can be taken in capsule form)

Echinacea

Helps to build up immune system and ward off viral infections (taken as tablets or in tincture form)

St John's wort

Particularly effective for anxiety, tension, depression neuralgia,sciatica, rheumatic pain (taken as tablets, drops or in a weaker dose as tea)

BACH FLOWER REMEDIES

Rescue remedy

In tincture form, a few drops in the mouth helps to reduce panic, anxiety, shock and the effects of grief. In cream form can be used on cuts, grazes, burns, bites and other types of skin irritation

Olive

For people lacking energy because of working too hard or who have over-exerted themselves

White chestnut

For those whose minds are so full of worries that they find it hard to concentrate on work or family

OTHER USEFUL REMEDIES

Aloe vera gel

To relieve the irritation of cuts, burns, sunburn and blisters, and to speed up healing

Vitamin E cream

Can be used for minor skin complaints and sunburn

organic skin- and haircare

Interest in eating organically to promote a healthier lifestyle has been increasing for some time now, but has the same consideration been given to the beauty and hair products and the cosmetics that we regularly buy? Skilled demonstrators convince us to buy expensive skincare products to improve our skin, but it is not often that we ask what they actually contain.

Skincare

The skin is the human body's largest organ and its important function is to provide a protective barrier from harmful substances such as pollution from the atmosphere, bacteria, foreign bodies and ultraviolet light. It also retains essential body fluids and regulates the body's temperature, so it needs to be treated with care. Unfortunately, as skin- and haircare products become more sophisticated, the number of unnatural ingredients they use is increasing, too. These unfortunately include pesticide residues, which are present in the air, evident in many waterways and in all mass-produced items. Since our skin is thought to absorb around 60 per cent of any cream or lotion that we use, we need to make ourselves more aware of what is contained in these beauty items. Apparently, many women's skins take in as much as 2kg (4½lb) of chemicals each year. The far healthier alternative for the consumer, and the environment, is to start buying organic ranges that are made from natural herbs, plants and scents.

The benefits of organic ranges

The number of companies making natural beauty and haircare products is increasing all the time, as is the number of ranges. Organic skincare companies are generally against animal testing in any form and will not use material from genetically modified crops. They also include organically grown plants and herbs as much as possible. Plant-based colorants, rather than synthetics, are used in lotions, powders and cosmetics – these are distinguished by the fact they start to fade on exposure to sunlight so they should be stored in dark conditions for maximum shelf life. Thought is given to packaging, too, with companies using reusable and recyclable bottles and packets.

Sometimes chemical names are seen as detergents in the shampoos or emulsifiers in moisturizers. Most of these are vegetable derived but occasionally chemical preservatives have to be added – this is normally stated – to give the long shelf life that consumers want.

Beauty ranges

Just because they are made organically, does not mean that the products are unsophisticated. One company boasts an organic skincare range containing extracts of rose and pure silk, and bath oils scented with lemon, rose and lavender. Carrot, calendula, jojoba and cocoa butter are included in an eye cream, while sandalwood, lemon, beeswax and olive oil help to make up one of their foundations. Some companies use only plants and herbs that are grown organically or biodynamically, the herbs collected just before sunrise when their life forces are believed to be at their strongest. Most companies producing organic skincare ranges avoid extensive mechanical manufacturing, doing many of the processes by hand.

Haircare

Normal hair products contain an overwhelming mixture of detergents, emulsifiers, thickening agents and preservatives, so that every time we wash our hair we absorb some through our skin, and pollute our drains with the rinsing water. Organic hair shampoos and conditioners made from mild foaming agents, natural plant extracts and essential oils are kind to both your hair and the environment. Or you can choose to use old-fashioned methods of keeping your hair gleaming and healthy – try rinsing with herbal infusions made by steeping camomile flowers (for fair hair), or elder leaves (for dark hair) in boiling water and letting it cool.

sourcing organic beauty ranges

The number of organic beauty ranges being produced has increased in recent years, but it is not always easy to find them on sale in big stores where there is still some resistance to sourcing and stocking ranges other than from the mainstream manufacturers. It is worth trying local healthfood and natural beauty shops, which often stock other products that have been made locally. Sometimes local producers sell from market stalls.

Where to buy

Healthfood stores are a good source of natural beauty ranges, but generally carry only a limited stock. Mail order can be a better option and the popular organic manufacturers (*see Organic Directory*) carry a good range of products, which can be ordered by post or phone, or through a website. The organic beauty ranges can be more expensive than others, because they are more labour intensive to manufacture. But when you consider that you will be reducing the number of toxic chemicals you are introducing into your skin or hair, they are well worth it.

The problem also is that some of the mainstream beauty product manufacturers have realized that there is a large, undeveloped market for healthier natural body products and they are only too willing to exploit it. Often a product is launched, claiming to be 'natural', but further investigation reveals it has only some natural ingredients that are generally not organic and sometimes refined. It is only when consumers protest that they are not getting what is being marketed and demand better quality and pricing that things start to change.

Branding is also a problem – the status appeal of owning a Chanel lipstick often wins when it comes to a brand that is naturally made, containing ingredients such as jojoba and rose hip extract. However, matters are slowly improving with many more people turning to organic beauty ranges, which contain no additives.

How the labelling works

At present, the labelling system in Europe for organic beauty ranges is not strictly enforced. Manufacturers are supposed to list all the ingredients used in their products but some of the information can still be confusing. Also, a product needs to include only 1 per cent of natural ingredients to be called 'natural' . So many of the 'natural' or 'pure' products that are on the market still contain as many as twenty chemicals!

Most of the respected companies producing organic beauty products state in their brochures and on their packaging that they do not test on animals or use animal ingredients. In addition, they state whether their products are suitable for vegans, whether they use natural

Ingredients to avoid

If you have a sensitive skin, are allergic to certain fragrances or suffer from asthma it is best to avoid the following ingredients, contained in both organic and ordinary beauty and haircare ranges.

Fragrances made from synthetic irritant chemicals

> Can cause skin sensitivity, asthma

Bergamot, orange or lime essential oil

> Can cause irritation in the sun, skin pigmentation

2-bromo-2-nitropropane-1, 3-diol Diazolidinyl urea (contained in preservatives)

> Both contain formaldehyde, which is carcinogenic and a neurotoxin

Methylchloroisothiazolinone Parabens (butyl, ethyl, methyl and propyl)

> Can cause allergic reactions or irritation

Diethanolamine (DEA) Triethanolamine (TEA)

> These are not a danger in themselves but are often mixed with nitrates, leading to formation of nitrosamines which are carcinogenic

Blue 1, Green 3, D&C Red 33, FD&C Yellow 5, FD&C Yellow 6

> These artificial colours are carcinogenic

Cosmetic grade lanolin

> Normal lanolin is fine, but this can be contaminated with pesticides such as DDT and dieldrin, which are carcinogenic

Paraphenylene (PPD) (in hair colorants)

> Can cause allergic reactions such as headaches, nausea, swelling, dizziness, itching, redness and fainting. Also linked to certain cancers

(most chart information from The Safe Shoppers Bible *by David Steinmann and Samuel S. Epstein, MD)*

fragrances or use some chemical preservatives, and they provide the proportion of natural herbs, oils and ingredients they use. Some will even give a full explanation of all the ingredients used.

making your own
beauty products

Making your own beauty products from natural ingredients is very fulfilling. They are simple and inexpensive to formulate and the live cultures and stimulating enzymes from fruits and yogurts that some contain bring life and vitality to your skin and hair.

Cleansers, toners and moisturizers

Everyone's skin tone is different. This is dependent on many factors: how well you take care of it, the type of air it is exposed to, lifestyle and diet, the amount of exercise you take, hormonal balance and age. A regular routine of cleansing, toning and moisturizing your skin will also help to keep it in good shape. Regular exfoliation with a body brush and ground rice or a mixture of bran, sea salt and yogurt every other day will also help to improve the skin texture on your body as it gets rid of dead skin cells, boosts your circulation and gives you fresher-looking skin.

Cleansers: You need to cleanse your facial skin daily with oils, milks or lotions to remove the grime that collects from the atmosphere, which can block pores and lead to spots. For a simple cleanser, smooth on some whole milk or yogurt with a tissue and wipe off with cotton wool. Using a face mask once a week helps to remove ingrained dirt.

Toners: remove any oily cleanser residue from the skin and help to restore the natural acid balance in the skin. To make a simple toner, squeeze some lemon juice or add a teaspoon of cider vinegar to a cup of water and apply to your skin with cotton wool.

Moisturizers: It is the water in the skin that keeps it looking good, rather than its oil content. However, it is the surface oil, sebum, that help cells to retain their moisture. Sebum can be unreliable in its efficiency so a moisturizing lotion can help maintain this balance.

Fruit face masks

The face masks below can be used on all skin types for basic deep cleansing. Clean the surface grime off your face first using a cleansing lotion, then apply one of the following 'recipes', leaving it on for 15 minutes, before rinsing it off.

Strawberry

Mash 3–6 strawberries into a pulp and apply to face and neck

Banana

Mash 1 banana with a teaspoon of organic honey, then smooth on to face and neck (particularly good for dry skins)

Avocado

Mix half a ripe avocado with a little honey and a drop of lemon juice then apply to face and neck

Cleansing lotions and moisturizers

Moisturizing creams can be more complicated to make than cleansing lotions but they do hydrate the skin quickly and effectively.

Cucumber cleanser (for oily skin)

½ ripe cucumber ● 150ml (¼ pint) whole milk

Blend the cucumber and milk in a liquidizer. Place in a medium plastic bottle and keep in the refrigerator – it will keep for a few days. Apply with cotton wool and wipe over face and neck

Yogurt and lime cleansing milk (for oily skin)

1 tbsp natural yogurt ● 1 tsp lime juice

Mix the ingredients together and apply with cotton wool

Avocado moisturizer

Blend a large avocado (with stone removed) in a liquidizer, then strain through a fine sieve to extract the oil. Apply to the face with cotton wool

Orange moisturizer

Save the peel of an orange. Cut it into sections and scour with a sharp object until you see the oil oozing out. Gently rub this oil over your face

Simple hair rinses

A hair rinse can enhance hair colours, restore its acid balance and make it shiny. Try rinsing your hair with a cup of cider vinegar for all types of hair, or mix the following oils with 1 litre (1¾ pints) of water to use as a final rinse.

For dark hair

2 drops rosemary essential oil ● 1 drop rosewood essential oil ● 1 drop lavender essential oil

For fair hair

2 drops camomile essential oil ● 2 drops lemon essential oil

eco-living

When you adopt the principle of living an organic lifestyle it affects every area of your life. In order to be truly healthy we need to embrace everything that leads to good health for ourselves and for the planet. Changing to an organic diet is an important step towards improving your well-being, but your home must also nurture both you and the environment. There are many ways to make your home as environmentally friendly as possible, and a healthy house, decorated with natural materials and conserving resources, can become a beautiful home, supporting every area of your life.

eco-friendly homes

Leading an eco-friendly lifestyle means being aware of all the choices that you make as a consumer. In just the same way as you may turn to an organic diet, you can choose household products, furnishings and appliances that do not harm the environment, and that are healthier for both you and your home.

Unseen home hazards
In order to make healthy options, try and avoid introducing potentially dangerous materials into your home, and be aware of the worst offenders.

Combustion gases
● Gas, paraffin, oil, coal and wood all release harmful by-products, particularly if combustion is inefficient and when ventilation is inadequate. Gas cookers and boilers must be serviced regularly or they can emit dangerous levels of carbon monoxide, carbon dioxide, nitric oxide and other dangerous vapours
● Unvented portable gas and paraffin heaters release gases as well as high humidity, leading to condensation problems. Only use in a well-ventilated space and never long term
● Wood and coal smoke contain pollutants, including carbon monoxide. These should go up the chimney but poorly designed flues and unswept chimneys can create problems

Volatile organic compounds (VOCs) in household products
● Hundreds of household products and building materials use formaldehyde – in medium-density fibreboard (MDF), paper products, furnishing fabrics, rugs and carpets. It can irritate skin, eyes, nose and throat. It is associated with breathing problems, headaches, nausea and fatigue, and may be carcinogenic
● Many pest control products and cleaning fluids as well as plastics contain organo-chlorines. They are potential carcinogens and persistent health and environmental hazards. PVC (polyvinyl chloride) and PCBs (polychlorinated biphenyls) are organochlorines
● Disinfectants and cleaning products often contain phenols or carbolic acids. Phenolic synthetic resins are found in hard plastics, paints, coatings and varnishes. Fungicides and wood preservatives often contain pentachlorophenol. Phenols may cause nausea, skin rashes and breathing difficulties

Particles
● Older properties may still have asbestos insulation and fireproofing. If so, have an expert remove and dispose of it carefully, as asbestos fibres are a serious health risk
● Most house dust is not a problem but poor ventilation and condensation encourage build-up of bacteria and moulds, as dust contains all sorts of micro-organisms including bacteria and viruses, moulds, spores and pollen
● Old paint can contain lead, and more modern paint contains titanium oxide. Be very careful when removing this paint, or call in an expert, as fumes are very toxic

Electromagnetic field (EMF) pollution
● Common electrical equipment – TVs, videos, computers, microwaves – give off persistent low-frequency electromagnetic waves. These can trigger allergies and headaches and raise stress levels, at the least. Use less electrical equipment, turn it off when not in use, and keep it away from sleeping spaces

Reasons for changing to an organic home

The home has always been a symbol of a safe and protective environment, and improved building standards and technologies have helped ensure that most homes are now safe. However, nowadays many of us live surrounded by chemical pollution. If you enter a new house you will find it often has a particular smell, which is usually a chemical fragrance from sprayed and treated woods and fabrics, glues and plastics. Increasingly, people are becoming susceptible to these unnatural substances, and the phrase 'sick building syndrome' has arisen. Many of us seem to be reacting to or developing allergies to the synthetic materials our homes are made from, to the chemical products we use daily and to the electrical fields that come off all the appliances we use. Western consumers are becoming increasingly aware that environmental factors can bring about disease.

Associations supporting a healthier home are most advanced in countries such as Germany. Here, the Baubiologie (building biology) movement developed in response to the massive rebuilding programme after the Second World War. Many people living in these new homes, made from synthetic materials, complained of depression, insomnia, allergies and higher incidences of cancer. Baubiologists have a holistic approach to the relationship between people and their buildings. They believe the house is like an organism, with its fabric being our third skin. They support siting the home and designing its interior so that it communes with nature and promotes our spiritual health. Their philosophy encourages the use of traditional materials and building methods, and advocates incorporating organic paint finishes and treatments.

key
concepts

An eco-friendly home tries to avoid unhealthy materials for their effect on personal and environmental health. It also consumes only the energy it needs and doesn't waste scarce resources. Many of us who live in the Western world are great consumers. We are enticed by advertising campaigns to try out all the latest household products without thinking of their cost to the environment. As well as avoiding chemicals, we should try and avoid buying products that generate waste through their packaging or disposal, we should make the most energy-conscious choices for fuel and lighting, and be careful of the amount of water we use.

Conserve resources

The keywords of an eco-friendly lifestyle are 'reduce, reuse, recycle'. Most of us could reduce our energy consumption drastically through some simple measures. All homes should be well insulated and weatherproofed, heating systems well serviced and never used when they're not needed – if a household heating thermostat is turned down by just 1°C, 10 per cent of energy is saved. If you are considering installing a new heating system look for the most energy-efficient, perhaps even turning to a renewable energy source such as solar power or eco-tricity.

In the Western world we take clean, piped tap water for granted without thinking of it as a scarce resource. A family of four uses around 155 litres (34 gallons) daily, one-third of which is used to flush the toilet. Water is a precious resource and the more we use, the more likely it is that supplies become polluted. It then takes more energy to clean them to recommended standards when this is still possible, yet conserving water is so easy. Never let a tap drip as this can waste around 4 litres (7 pints) a day, recycle bath and dish-washing water for use in the garden, and try and take showers, which use only 40 per cent of the water needed for a bath.

Waste less

Much of what we buy today is packaged, and every year each household in the US and the UK produces an estimated 1 tonne of rubbish. Although facilities for recycling items such as glass, paper and cans are now common, plastics are still a problem as many are not biodegradable. Waste is rapidly becoming a global problem as landfill sites fill up and we need to reduce our waste drastically. It is estimated that at least 40 per cent of any household's rubbish could be composted, providing a new resource for the land, and most of the rest could be recycled. If you choose your products carefully you may not need to send anything to a landfill tip.

Avoid plastics

Plastics are made from oil, itself a limited resource, through an energy-intensive process whereby more scarce resources are consumed. Around 30 per cent of plastics in the UK are used in packaging, which is used once and then discarded to landfill sites. Although plastic recycling facilities are becoming more common, some plastics will not recycle and the process is complicated and expensive. It is much more sensible to avoid plastics in the first place.

Reduce, reuse, recycle
By reusing, reducing or recycling products in our homes, we can economize and lessen the environmental damage.

- Create less waste by buying only what you need
- Do not buy heavily packaged goods
- Try and avoid purchasing plastics as they are difficult to recycle
- Reuse plastic carrier bags or ask for paper bags when you shop
- Transform kitchen biodegradable waste into compost for your garden

- Use glass bottles that can be recycled easily rather than plastic
- Recycle all aluminium and steel cans – wash them first and squash them flat
- Recycle newspapers, paper and cardboard
- Recycle clothes, toys, shoes and materials at charity shops, textile banks or jumble sales
- Recycle old furniture through kerbside pick-up schemes or community projects
- Always try and source reclaimed building materials – bricks, stone slabs, tiles, beams and doors – from architectural salvage yards and junk yards

- When you do buy new, take into account the resources it took to produce the item, and try and buy local products wherever possible

Hazardous waste
- Take oil paints, solvents, garden chemicals and other items to your local hazardous waste collection centre, or check with your council. Some will degas refrigerators and recycle fluorescent tubes
- Deposit car oil cans, car batteries and transmission fluid at a recycling centre
- Dry out water-based paints and dispose of them with household waste

the natural home – room by room

When you adopt ecological principles, your whole attitude towards your home may change. You will probably discover that there are practices and products in your home that you can change in order to live a healthier and more organic lifestyle. There is no need to make a whole heap of changes all at once, every small step you make towards a more natural lifestyle is a positive one. Even a simple change such as introducing natural colours and scents, more plants, a shower or a recycling box, is important.

First steps

Look around your home carefully and think about the materials and appliances it contains. See how you can make gradual improvements. Study each room and see how you can change items to bring in more natural materials – ideally furniture, flooring and fabrics should be natural, not synthetic; paints and varnishes should be organic, and appliances should conserve rather than waste energy. There may be simple steps you can take to conserve energy and improve the overall air quality by reducing chemical inputs – try to avoid chemical cleaners but opt instead for eco-friendly ones that are safer for your health and biodegrade when you dispose of them. Try and simplify your home, too. Removing pockets of clutter always makes a home feel more relaxing and creates a vibrant atmosphere, as your home should feed your mental as well as your physical health.

The living areas

Often seen as the most important room in the home, this is the room where you can relax by yourself or with the family or you may entertain friends. Unfortunately, its contents can too often work against us. Many living rooms have sofas and chairs made from MDF or particle board, and cushions are often filled with foam and covered in synthetic materials, or treated with stain-retardant sprays. All of these may contain harmful chemicals, which can offgas into the indoor air. Gradually replace any such furnishings with products made from natural alternatives – wooden furniture, upholstery and cushions made from naturally dyed wool and cotton fibres, and using organic cotton with kapok, down or feather fillings. Ask your supplier or timber merchant in order to be sure that the wood comes from sustainable managed woodland, and do not buy wood from tropical forests. Or choose from wide ranges of oriental-style chairs, tables and sofas made from wicker, cane, bamboo, rattan or seagrass. Before rushing to buy new furniture, first try to find and reuse older furniture and furnishings but do make absolutely sure that you are not then unwittingly introducing hazardous chemical finishes into your living room.

As for beneath your feet, carpets are often synthetic or chemically treated. The healthiest flooring is natural wood (from a sustainable source) or tiles covered with woollen or cotton rugs, or natural linoleum made from cork and linseed oil. But if you want wall-to-wall carpeting, choose wool and preferably woven carpet, which doesn't need the glue required by tufted carpets. Check with your supplier to be sure that the wool used in the carpet is free from pesticide residues (particularly organochlorines) and has not been treated with fungicides. Floor coverings from plant fibres such as jute, hemp, sisal and coir are also very healthy and adaptable, but all flooring should be kept clean and dry so that you don't get a build-up of dust and moulds. Use natural rubber underlay and avoid carpet adhesives that may emit VOCs.

Electrical equipment such as stereos, TVs, videos and computers all give off EMFs and low-level radiation, which can adversely affect health. Ideally, these should be in a separate room to a living room, but space doesn't often permit this. So make sure you sit a minimum of 2.5m (8ft) away from a television – making sure that children don't squat right in front – as radiation levels decrease with distance. Also, don't work or play too long on a computer. Plants such as peace lilies (*Spathiphyllum* spp.) or spider plants *Chlorophytum elatum* can help to clean the air around electrical appliances.

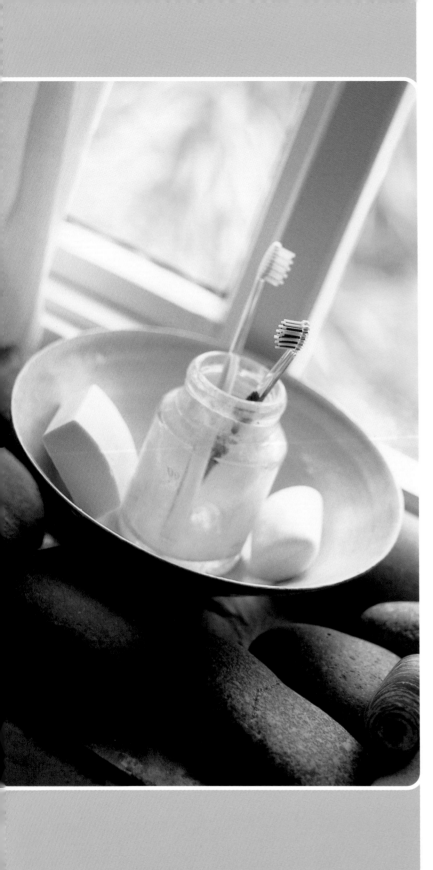

Bedrooms

Humans spend around one-third of their lives in bed, and restful sleep is a vital healing process, enabling us to awake refreshed and rejuvenated for a new day. It is therefore important to choose a good bed. Metal-framed beds are liable to attract magnetism, which can disrupt your sleep, so choose a solid wooden bed (from a sustainable source). A slatted bed is better than one with a solid base as it allows air to circulate to the mattress. Look for mattresses made from untreated cotton or the slightly more pricey latex, and find a good ergonomic one that supports your spine. A natural down or organic cotton-filled duvet and pillows with linen or cotton covers and sheets will encourage good sleep.

The position of your bed may be important. The earth has natural terrestrial magnetic fields to which life is attuned. Some houses are built above fissures or cracks in the earth or watercourses where the magnetic fields may be disturbed. Long-term exposure to this distorted energy field may lead to a condition known as 'geopathic stress', where an individual can become tired, stressed and generally unwell. So, to avoid any potential problems, align your bed north–south to place you in line with the earth's natural magnetic field. Do not use a computer in your bedroom, and try to keep electrical equipment in the room to the minimum.

If at all possible, invest in natural, untreated furnishings and fabrics in your bedroom, as vapours given off by synthetic furnishings can cause sleeplessness, irritability and exhaustion. This is particularly vital in children's bedrooms so you don't store up problems for the future.

The kitchen

This should be a welcoming room, but a modern kitchen can be rather wasteful of energy and full of chemical pollutants. MDF kitchen units are common but undesirable, particularly as food prepared in a chemically tainted environment may pick up traces of chemicals. Look at natural, rather than synthetic, materials for floors and work surfaces. Sustainable woods such as beech, maple and oak treated with natural varnishes or waxes create a durable surface. Granite, although expensive, makes a long-lasting work surface, while slate or quarry tiles add a rugged texture to the floor.

Change from chemical cleaners and detergents to environmentally sound ones (*see page 143*) to avoid polluting the air, the water and the environment. As well as good food storage space, make sure you have adequate storage areas for recycling waste products such as bottles, paper, cardboard and cans. When you need to replace kitchen appliances, make sure you choose eco-friendly models of cookers, washing machines, dishwashers, refrigerators and freezers.

The bathroom

A calming sanctuary away from the outside world, the bathroom should cater for relaxation and pleasure as well as hygiene. Soaking in warm or hot water is a wonderful way to unwind, but be aware of water conservation and take a shower whenever possible as this uses less than half the amount of water as a bath. Toilets flush away huge quantities of water, so if you need a new one choose a low-flush model, or even go for a composting version which uses no water at all. Otherwise, place a brick or similar object in your cistern so that it doesn't fill up with more water than it needs to flush – this simple water-saving measure can save a family of four at least 20 litres (4½ gallons) of water in a single day.

Never lay carpet in a bathroom as it attracts bacteria and moulds. Instead choose natural linoleum, tiles or wood, which is well sealed. Use cotton shower curtains, and unbleached toilet paper. Walls should be painted with a natural paint that breathes, or tiled so that they can be easily wiped down. And always use natural materials for all your bathroom accessories: cotton mats and towels, cotton flannels, sea sponges and hemp or sisal mitts. Choose non-chemical bathroom cleaners, and biodegradable cosmetics and bathing products such as soaps made from natural plant extracts.

a healthy environment

It is not just the materials that you use in your home that influence it. There are other more subtle forces at work as well. When you walk into a truly ecological home, you are immediately aware of something special. The space feels clear and uncluttered, the air feels clear and clean and you can breathe deeply, there is plenty of natural daylight and the colours, forms and spaces all please your senses. You feel more alive and positive.

Unseen energies

Dowsers have always known about earth energies, and geomancy is an ancient art – siting habitations and sacred places to align with particular energy spots. It is more recently, however, that scientists have begun to look at the way that natural electromagnetic radiation from the earth varies in intensity at different places, and the effect this may have on health. Some houses seem to be built in more auspicious places than others, but there are ways to make the most of any situation through awareness of the way that energies flow through a building. The ancient Chinese system of *feng shui* in particular can be very useful for deciding on ways to create and maintain healthy interior spaces.

Feng shui works on the principle that spirals of energy need to flow freely through the home for harmony and well-being. When piles of clutter block the hallway, accumulate on the stairs, in the kitchen or around and under the bed this energy flow becomes blocked, creating stagnant areas. The energy moves on sluggishly, having a detrimental effect on the occupants, making them feel confused and unable to move on and let new things into their lives. Clutter is things you no longer love or use – recycle as much as possible so that other people can benefit.

Air

Buildings sealed for heat conservation and those with central heating systems may harbour toxins that contribute to 'sick building syndrome' (*see page 129*). The best way of clearing the air is to throw open the windows, but in a busy city this may lead to increased pollution. If this is the case, an ionizer is an inexpensive and effective basic air purifier. It transforms heavy positive ions in the air, which occur when air is polluted, into negatively charged ones, which are energizing.

Green plants such as spider plants *Chlorophytum elatum* help improve air quality, absorbing VOCs and other pollutants. Essential oils of certain aromatic plants also clear the air and actually enter the bloodstream through the skin or lungs to invigorate the brain. The oils can be diffused through special lamps. Herbs such as sage have been used by Native American Indians for centuries to cleanse and invigorate spaces.

Light and colour

Houses need natural light since changes in intensity of light are important to human rhythms and affect our health and well-being. Any healthy home should take advantage of natural light wherever possible. Use direct light for kitchens and workrooms, especially where it is essential for safety, and use reflected and diffused lighting in more intimate spaces. If you work indoors under artificial lighting, choose full spectrum lighting, which contains the same balance of colours as natural sunlight.

Light and shade affect colour in many ways. In pale-coloured rooms natural light and reflections will make the colours vary subtly and as the spectrum of sunlight changes during the day the colours in a room will seem to alter. Take account of these qualities of natural light when you plan your decorations and furnishings, and also the way in which different colours have different effects on people. However there are certain fairly general rules: red makes rooms look smaller and keeps us alert; orange is also stimulating, so use these colours in activity rooms. Yellows and greens can be rather unsettling, while a warm blue room will be calming and relaxing.

energy conservation

Many old homes were built with little regard to the energy they used, and modern ones often do not have as many energy-saving features as they could. However, houses or apartments are very adaptable and even making small adjustments such as draughtproofing old windows, or changing to energy-efficient light bulbs can make a real difference.

The right heating

An open fire always looks welcoming in a room but it is a less efficient form of heat than a gas-fired central heating system that is kept properly maintained. An old gas boiler can start to leak carbon monoxide, nitrogen dioxide and carbon dioxide into the room, so have it serviced yearly and make sure it has the correct ventilation to the outside. Wood-burning stoves or boilers are a good option where firewood is easy to come by locally as they use less energy and release low levels of harmful gases into the atmosphere, but do ensure you have the flues checked regularly and swept. Whatever heating system you choose for your home, use it only when you have to; a timed system wastes less energy when you're not there, and to keep bills lower in the winter set the thermostat at around 16–18°C/60–65°F.

Solar heating

If you are installing a new heating system consider solar power, a way of converting sunlight into energy. This works best if your house faces south or gets a lot of sun, but heat will come through even on cloudy days and transfer to your hot water tank. Hot water bills can in fact be halved by installing these panels, but it needs to be a twenty-year plan because they are costly to install. If your house doesn't have the right aspect, you could consider photovoltaic solar panels, which are movable panels that can be sited to catch maximum sun. Solar systems are most efficient in a cooler climate if you back them up with low-emission wood-burning stoves.

Improving insulation

Good insulation is fundamental to any energy-conscious home. By ensuring your loft and the roof space are well insulated, around 20 per cent of heating costs can be saved. Fitting cavity wall insulation can reduce heat loss by up to 60 per cent. Conversely, another 20 per cent is often lost through badly fitting doors and windows, so check these thoroughly and seal them with draughtproofing materials. Double-glazing helps greatly with heat loss, as well as aiding noise reduction, too. Check for other places where heat could be being lost – floorboards, skirtings, around old fireplaces or openings – and seal them appropriately.

- Fit reflective foil behind radiators to conserve heat
- Have a water meter fitted and check your water consumption
- Boiling a kettle half instead of wholly full, just once a day, saves enough electricity to run a TV for an hour
- Save washing for a full load and use an economy cycle
- Replacing a boiler over fifteen years old can save 15 per cent on fuel bills
- Insulate your hot water tank and all your heating pipes

Lighting

Many of us leave lights needlessly switched on in rooms we are not using. This wastes a high amount of electricity and the tungsten filament bulbs commonly used also give off heat. These light bulbs are incandescent, meaning that light is generated when the electrical current passes through a thin metal wire, which becomes hot and gives out light. Only about 10 per cent of the electrical energy is converted to light and the rest burns as heat. Instead of such light bulbs, fit compact fluorescent lamps (CFLs), energy-efficient light bulbs and fluorescent strip lights, which are eight to ten times more efficient than other bulbs because they are made to produce light not heat. The fluorescent tube in a strip light absorbs ultraviolet radiation when mercury in the tube reacts to an electrical charge. The bulbs will last nearly ten times as long as a conventional one. However, they do not work with dimmer switches nor some timing devices.

using natural
DIY products

Decorating is one of the most popular areas of home improvement, and most of us get involved in it at some stage. Avoid solvent-based synthetic products and choose instead from the wide ranges of paints, varnishes, wall-papers, glues and stains that are water-based or organic and plant-based. These have just as many colours and textures as the other ranges.

Paints

Most conventional oil paint ranges are derived from petro-chemicals and contain synthetic colour dyes, solvents to make the paint flow (some of which are believed to be carcinogenic), acrylic resin binders, emulsifiers and thinners. The solvents contain VOCs, such as xylene, epoxy, toluene and benzene, which emit gas while in use and when drying. Even high-sheen, water-based paints give off volatile compounds; the low-sheen ones have less toxicity but still contain some chemicals.

The only truly natural alternatives are organic paints. The equivalent to oil paints are natural resin paints, which normally contain linseed oil, plant resins and other ingredients such as chalk, indigo and aromatic oils. They have microporous properties, which means that they will resist water but let some water vapour through the wall to stop paint from blistering. Sometimes the paint takes longer to dry than conventional paints. Water-based gloss paints are also being introduced.

Organic emulsion paint is available in a wide range of earthy and vibrant colours, or you can buy white and add coloured pigments of your choice. The paint covers well and has an attractive finish. Some organic distemper, or water-based paints, are thinned with milk casein – these paints are washable. Mixed colour ranges are also available in casein paints but it is most usual to buy a white base and add pigments or use plant colour washes to create special finishes.

Paint thinners

Paint thinners are used to clean paintbrushes. Conventional choices, turpentine substitute and white spirit, both contain petrochemicals, so a better choice is pure turpentine, which comes from a resinous oil. It is available from builders' suppliers. Alternatively, there is a natural paint thinner made from citrus peel, which can be suitable for people who react to turpentine substitutes; or use thinners made from pure plant oil available from organic suppliers.

Wood products, varnishes and waxes

Most commercial wood treatments contain toxic arsenics or creosote. Sensible alternatives include a borax wood impregnation treatment, which is fungicidal and insecticidal. A wood-pitch treatment of resin-oil and beechwood distillate is available for exterior wood protection.

Most wood sealants are synthetic preparations based on polyurethane and can cause allergies. It is far better to use natural resin-oil primers for interior and exterior woodwork, cork and clay. Synthetic varnishes can also contain solvents and traces of lead, so use varnishes based on natural resins from tropical trees, plus linseed oil and thinners. Shellac and manila are excellent. Floors and furniture also benefit from treatment with natural oil resins, add natural stains and pigments when required.

Pure beeswax has a pleasant scent and adds a glowing sheen to interior wood surfaces, bringing out the natural grain. Liquid beeswax is ideal for wood, cork, stone and clay; mixed beeswax and plant waxes are equally effective and have a very pleasant scent.

Wallpaper

Most types of wallpaper are ecologically sound as they are mainly made from recycled or sustainable wood pulp; some are hand-printed with natural dyes. More unusual natural alternatives to wallpaper include using interesting wrapping paper, or hanging hessian and fabric panels on the wall. Try to avoid vinyl wallpapers because, although waterproof, they are covered in a thin layer of vinyl, which can give off nasty vapours. Hang all wallpapers with organic glue, such as methyl cellulose, as normal paste has fungicides and adhesives that can irritate the skin.

conventional
cleansers

Nowadays, in pursuit of a spotless home, we use a mixture of detergents, polishes, bleaches, disinfectants and other products that contain potentially harmful chemicals. It may not always be noticeable how they are affecting us, but people with heightened sensitivity can suffer from headaches, breathing problems or skin irritations. Chemicals can also end up in water supplies and in our ground water, so it is always best to buy natural products that biodegrade.

Safety standards

While in theory most common cleaning products have been officially approved as 'safe', they still contain a mixture of toxins that can pollute the environment and harm us. Environmental campaigners, Friends of the Earth, have come up with the following five key policies for the sustainable use of chemicals:

● A full right to know, including what chemicals are present in products
● A deadline by which all chemicals on the market must have their safety independently assessed. All uses of a chemical should be approved and demonstrated to be safe beyond reasonable doubt
● A phasing out of persistent or bioaccumulative chemicals (chemicals that stick around in the environment or accumulate in our bodies)
● A requirement to substitute less safe chemicals with safer alternatives
● A commitment to stop all releases to the environment of hazardous substances by 2020

© 2000 Friends of the Earth

Home-made alternatives

There are plenty of natural alternatives we can use in our homes (see opposite). Either choose from the wide range of eco-friendly products available in stores or go back to basics. For example, clean stained kitchen surfaces with lemon juice or soapy water and a little washing soda, while vinegar makes a good bleach and can descale items such as kettles and showerheads.

Unassuming plants can be as powerful as any strong chemicals. The leaves of the common wood sorrel *Oxalis acetosella* make a natural bleach thanks to the high levels of oxalic acid in the plant. Make a strong infusion, steep for an hour or two then reboil and use. The juice from its leaves will remove rust spots and ink stains from linen or cotton. Other useful plants include walnut and hazelnut, which make excellent furniture polishes when you rub the kernel's cut surface over the furniture due to the oil released from the nut. Also, light scorch marks on rugs can be removed by rubbing with the cut edge of a raw onion.

Natural cleaners

For a healthier home, consider using natural alternatives instead of the toxic chemicals found in many cleaners.

Washing detergents and conditioners contain bleaching agents, phosphates and petrochemical surfactants

Alternatives: Biodegradable products free of phosphates; borax is a good stain remover, vinegar a good fabric softener

Washing-up liquids contain water-polluting phosphates, artificial dyes and petrochemicals

Alternatives: Phosphate-free products with natural ingredients, liquid soap and lemon juice, herbal vinegar for grease, washing soda for hard water

Bleaches and scourers contain sodium hypochlorite, which releases irritating toxic fumes, and bleach and ammonia, both of which destroy the good bacteria that breaks down sewage

Alternatives: Use biodegradable cleaners – baking soda or borax and water paste is good for cleaning baths. Lemon juice will bleach stubborn stains

Toilet cleaners contain hydrochloric acid

Alternatives: Cleaners with safer acetic acid; pour vinegar down toilet, leave overnight and brush well. Or do the same but mix with flour, or brush with baking soda or borax and lemon juice to clean and disinfect

Floor and furniture polishes contain strong chemicals such as phenol, nitrobenzene, methyl ethylene

Alternatives: Natural beeswax polishes, or two parts vegetable oil to one part lemon juice or white vinegar

Disinfectants contain carbolic acid and benzalkronium chloride

Alternatives: Tea tree, lavender and thyme essential oils are natural disinfectants

Air fresheners contain ingredients such as naphthalene, phenol, which can cause headaches, and paradichlorobenzene

Alternatives: Use dried herbs or flowers. Spray room with a mister filled with water and a few drops of stimulating essential oil such as citrus, lemon or basil

'green' electrical
appliances

The modern home contains many labour-saving gadgets to help ease our busy lives. Making your home into a natural home does not mean that you need to do without such machines, but use appliances carefully and think about switching to models with energy- and eco-saving features.

Cookers

Gas is environmentally the best choice of fuel for cooking since most methods of generating electricity produce three times as much carbon dioxide. If you do cook electric, use efficient cooking methods: a pressure cooker reduces cooking time, while a steamer can cook several items at once; always put lids on your pans and try and cook several things together in the oven.

Energy-conscious refrigeration

When buying a new refrigerator or freezer, try to find an energy-efficient model that is completely free of CFCs, HFCs and HCFCs, and that runs on less than 350kw/h annually (150kw/h for refrigerators).

- Do not buy a refrigerator or freezer that is bigger than you need or you will be using energy to cool empty space
- Place your refrigerator/freezer in a cool place for best performance
- Keep the coils at the back dust-free to prevent higher energy consumption
- Defrost regularly and check door seals for leaks

Refrigerator/freezers

Some older refrigerator or freezer models have a harmful impact on the environment, releasing now banned chloro-fluorocarbon (CFC) gas, which is believed to be destroying the ozone layer. Hydrochlorofluorocarbons (HCFCs), used as a coolant in older machines, are also banned for the same reason. Hydrofluorocarbons (HFCs) are being promoted to replace these other chemicals but are not ideal either as they, too, are strong greenhouse gases.

Washing machines

Use these invaluable appliances wisely as their use currently accounts for about 13 per cent of domestic energy consumption in the UK, using about 12 per cent of domestic water. Always save up washing until you have a full load, and preferably run the machine on economy electricity tariff at night. When buying a new washing machine, choose one with economy features such as eco-programmes for wash cycles and increased spin speeds, which take more moisture out of the clothes and decrease the drying time. Also look for a low-wattage machine and check that it is not cold-fill only as this uses more power.

EU labelling

Energy labelling is now mandatory on all appliances and these should appear with the sales brochure. Ecolabels (or their equivalent) are voluntary and manufacturers have to apply for them.

● The voluntary EU Ecolabel was introduced in 1992 by the European Commission and assesses appliances for their impact on the environment

● The European Ecolabel is voluntary and it sets limits for water consumption and energy and detergent loss. Some manufacturers promote the ecological features of their machines, while other companies seem less willing to provide clear information

● The EU label for washing machines will give its wash performance, spin speed and its noise levels

● On refrigerator/freezers energy efficiency is graded by the manufacturer from the best at 'A' through to the least efficient at 'G'

Dishwashers

Modern dishwashers actually use less water and energy than washing up by hand – often less than 20 litres (4½ gallons). The machines will also monitor how dirty the water is and whether it can be recycled for another wash. They will recycle heat between cycles, and use only air to dry the dishes. It is tempting to use the dishwasher on a half load and prewash dirty dishes, but this wastes water and it is more energy efficient to do full loads and rinse crockery and utensils under the tap.

grow your own

If you're interested in organic living then pursuing organic practices in the garden will allow you to make a very personal and worthwhile contribution to the environment. The old adage 'every little helps' could not be more appropriate. By taking responsibility for your own little patch of land you will help to minimize ecological waste and damage. Ethics aside, the payback in terms of productivity is enormous. Organic gardening is simply the most rewarding way to create a beautiful and productive garden full of diverse wildlife. What could possibly be more worthwhile than that?

the
principles

The benefits of organic gardening are manifold – whether you are motivated by ethics, economy, gastronomy or health. In essence, good organic gardening starts with the soil – get that right and all else will follow. Healthy soil promotes vigorous and fruitful plant growth. This lures wildlife into the garden and, in time, natural controls will operate – pests and diseases will be controlled naturally instead of being eradicated artificially.

Earth matters

Any professional grower wishing to adopt organic status requires certification (*see page 18*). However, the soil is the starting point for any organic gardener, whatever size their plot of land. Healthy plant growth depends on soil quality, therefore what you put into the soil you will get back. Plants do not thrive on a starvation diet any more than we do.

Good organic soil is rich in decomposing organic matter, called humus, and it is teeming with micro-organisms and insects. There are a range of organic materials that you can incorporate into your soil. Compost is made by recycling garden and household waste, transforming the ubiquitous heap of green rubbish into valuable, nutrient-rich plant food. Leaf mould, made from rotted fallen leaves, is less rich in nutrients but it bulks up compost and makes it go further. Manure from horses, chickens and pigs must be well rotted before it is incorporated into the soil. Remember that manure is not by its nature organic – it must come from an organic source.

Soil conditioning

Composting is a must for the keen organic gardener. Quite apart from it being a cost-effective way to improve the condition of your soil, it simply makes no sense to dispose of green household waste along with the rest of your rubbish, when you could benefit from recycling it at home. In environmental terms, the case for recycling green waste is even stronger – it is a small personal contribution that we can all make to reduce unnecessary waste disposal.

As well as making your own compost, you could grow your own 'green manure' (*see page 155*). This is a crop grown purely to nurture and feed the soil. The benefits of 'green manure' are twofold; it protects the soil structure from overexposure to the elements – too much sun or heavy rain is no more beneficial to the soil than it is for our skin – and it feeds the soil when it is incorporated into it.

The plants that thrive in such fertile soil will attract more insects. These will, in turn, encourage other forms of wildlife – such as birds, frogs and hedgehogs – which will, as a natural lifecycle consequence, feed your soil with their own individual forms of fertilizer! As the balance of nature returns to your garden and your soil quality gradually improves, so your plants will, in turn, become healthier and more resistant to diseases.

Good gardening

By taking up organic techniques, gardening also becomes less stressful and more productive. Instead of trying to bend nature to our will, we work with nature to find plants that thrive in our own particular region without labour-intensive and environmentally damaging chemical attention. Gardening is not difficult. Seeds sow themselves naturally and plants will try to grow in the most adverse conditions. Given good soil, primed with plenty of organic matter, plants will thrive. But organic gardening also means good garden management.

Sensible plant selection is the secret behind any great planting scheme. Don't struggle to grow acid-loving plants like rhododendrons (*Rhododendron* spp.) or heathers (*Erica* spp.) in chalky soil when their natural habitat is an acid soil. Why attempt to change the natural balance of a perfectly good soil to sustain a plant that isn't at home in your environment? Organic gardening is not about battling with nature to come out on top – it is about working *with* it. Grow plants that naturally thrive in your area. If you are desperate to grow a plant that struggles in your kind of soil you may be able to create a special environment, with the right soil, by using containers or by building a raised bed.

Pests

Organic gardeners respect the rich diversity of wildlife in their garden. Not all creatures in gardens are pests – indeed an animal or insect only becomes a pest when its lifestyle affects our plants adversely. It is perfectly possible to deal effectively with pests and diseases without the use of chemicals.

The whole cycle is interdependent and those pesky caterpillars that munch holes in your precious greens will metamorphose into beautiful pollinating butterflies. Organic gardeners must aim to control but not eradicate pests. Eradication upsets the balance of the whole eco-system. That is why it is so important that your garden should attract as great a diversity of wildlife as possible.

Chemical controls are not selective in what they kill. If you want to wipe out an aphid infestation with a pesticide, for example, it will kill ladybirds and hoverflies as well. This may not appear to present an immediate problem, but with fewer such predators in the garden your next aphid infestation and the ones after that will be increasingly severe. With no natural pest control in operation, things can get rapidly out of hand and it can take several years for the natural balance in your garden to be restored. So try to avoid using pesticides.

There are numerous systems for dealing with pests and disease that the organic gardener can call upon, from methods of biological control – introducing a predator or parasite that will naturally rid you of a pest – to sensible plant selection, such as choosing a variety of vegetable that has good resistance to specific pests. Basic measures such as hygiene and crop rotation will have an enormous impact, too. Some families of plants are highly susceptible to certain soil-borne pests and diseases – if you plant them in the same spot every year problems will inevitably build up in the soil. By rotating crops, on a four-yearly basis, it is possible to avoid any trouble.

Hygiene is critical, and many pests and diseases will over-winter in fallen leaves and fruit. Don't panic at the first sign of a spot or wilt on a leaf. Investigate the cause – often, simply removing infected leaves will be effective enough. It is worth investing in a specialist book on pests and diseases so that you can identify any problems early on. Companion plants, which lure desirable predators to an area or which serve as a decoy for the main crop, are another weapon the organic gardener can utilize. It seems absurdly simple as a system but successful companion planting can be spectacularly successful. Hoverfly larvae are more useful in controlling aphids than ladybirds. The adults are attracted to yellow flowers, therefore by planting yellow companion flowers close to any plants that suffer from regular aphid attacks you can sit back and let nature deal with the problem for you.

Organic by design

Even the overall garden layout has implications for the organic gardener. Introduce more trees, shrubs and hedges and new wildlife habitats are created. A diverse planting scheme will attract more insects both to pollinate flowers and eat those pests. If you attract the insects, the birds, bats and hedgehogs will follow. Nesting boxes, bat roosts and hedgehog dens will make your garden even more attractive. Water features will make that environment more appealing to wildlife, too – notably to slug-hungry frogs and toads.

Going green

It is important not to overlook the importance of what you buy to plant in your garden. The purist would argue that all seed should be organic. It *is* now possible to obtain organic vegetable and herb seeds. Organic flower seeds are less common, although some companies do offer untreated seeds. Try to make your own organic growing media, and steer clear of peat. Wild flower seeds should be native in origin and bulbs should never be taken from the wild. Avoid using moss to line hanging baskets, use wool or other recycled materials instead.

There are no hard-and-fast rules as yet, regarding which landscaping materials are most suitable for organic, eco-friendly gardeners, but it obviously makes common sense to source materials locally. Try to recycle materials where possible – use timber from sustainable sources and avoid using any wood preservatives or treated timber. Avoid plastic items wherever possible, opting instead for materials from renewable sources.

planning an
organic garden

The first step in going organic is to plan your garden. It's important to make a list of your expectations and to be realistic about what you can achieve in your given space. However small your plot, make room to grow some of your own produce as nothing can beat the flavour of home-grown new potatoes, a freshly picked lettuce or a small bowl of strawberries.

Thinking ahead

The word to remember when planning your organic garden is 'balance'. The organic garden plan will demand that you consider the needs of wildlife and your soil as an integral part of this scheme, as well as the usual garden requirements of seating areas, paths and flowerbeds.

Draw a plan of the boundaries of your garden and mark in features such as trees and water features. Consider the structure as the bare bones of the garden. Think about how you use the garden and don't overlook things like washing lines and compost heaps. Less visually appealing items can be concealed behind a bamboo screen or willow hurdle.

If you want to grow fruit or vegetables you should set aside suitable areas of the garden (*see pages 158–163*). The soil here will need to be easily worked, with a good nutritional content, and growing space will be required for your crops. A beautifully worked vegetable plot is every bit as appealing as the lush flower border, and any wise gardener will advise cultivating flowers in the fruit and vegetable patch for more than mere aesthetics. Flowers next to crops can act as decoys, distracting pests from main crops, repelling insects with their perfume or attracting predators.

While it is desirable to keep hard landscaping to a minimum you must be able to move around the garden with ease. Organic gardens need to be user-friendly. If you are recycling household waste you must be able to get to your compost heap easily – wading through thick mud daily will prove a very real disincentive. Be realistic about areas of heavy traffic and plan paths accordingly (*see pages 174–175*). A comfortable width for a path is 1m (3ft), which will readily accommodate a wheelbarrow.

You will doubtless want to sit and gaze on your organic estate, so a pleasant seating area, surrounded by perfumed flowers, will provide a peaceful haven, as well as attracting pollinating insects. Storage needs to be considered, too, for tidily kept tools and precious seeds.

Water for life

The appeal of water features in any garden design is well known, but in the organic garden they have even more significance. From the diminutive bird-bath to the larger scale they attract wildlife, which is essential to help control pests and improve fertility. It is important that any water feature has a sloping edge to allow easy access for wildlife, but remember that water features are a real danger to young children and should be fenced off for safety.

Water shortages affect many gardens in the summer months but you can take measures to collect and conserve as much water as possible. Although mulching and general organic practices help the soil to absorb and retain moisture, water will always be required. Water butts sited next to the house will collect rain falling from the roof, and you can divert water from baths, showers and sinks for recycling in the garden – this is known as 'grey' water. However, only divert water if you use chemical-free detergents and soaps, and do not store grey water for more than a few days or it can become smelly and attract insects, even though it will be in a covered barrel.

Grass

Lawns provide a wonderful green and entirely natural surface, a perfect foil for flowerbeds, but they need to be maintained and if they get out of condition they can be very labour intensive. A kitchen garden criss-crossed with paths might serve you better than a little used expanse of green. Alternatively, choose a hardwearing low-maintenance meadow grass, and mow paths through it.

building a
healthy garden

The first step to a fertile garden is to determine what kind of soil you have and its acid/alkaline balance. The ideal soil for growing most plants is about pH 6.5. Soil pH kits are readily available in shops and garden centres and can tell you the pH of your own particular soil. A pH of 7 indicates a neutral soil, anything below 7 indicates an acid soil, while a reading above 7 will indicate an alkaline soil. It is possible to slightly raise or lower your soil pH levels – if you add sulfur to the soil it makes it more acid, while the addition of lime will make it more alkaline.

Cultivation

The starting point of soil improvement for most gardeners is weed control. Weeds compete with cultivated plants and can also harbour pests and diseases. Digging thoroughly is highly effective to remove weeds but you should not dig every year as digging disturbs the natural balance and structure of the soil. Instead, apply mulches to the surface for worms to drag down and incorporate within the soil.

Mulching

A mulch is a material applied to the top of the soil, which can smother weeds, condition the soil, keep weed seeds off cultivated soil or inhibit moisture loss. Impenetrable mulches such as old carpet or black polythene suppress and smother weeds, but they can take a year or more to clear a patch of weeds effectively. Porous plastic

membranes are excellent for keeping areas weed-free after clearing. Plant through slits in these mulches. Paper and cardboard can be used, but must be weighted down with another loose mulch such as bark or cocoa shell. Compost, manure or even a few centimetres of grass clipping all make good, conditioning surface mulches and, while they won't control weeds, they will improve the quality of the soil.

When weeding, try to get every piece of the root out since small pieces of vigorous perennial weeds left in the soil can sprout new plants. The worst perennial offenders include bindweed *Calystegia sepium*, couch grass *Elymus repens* and ground elder *Aegopodium podagraria*. Stinging nettles *Urtica dioica* are a perennial nuisance but help make nutritious compost.

The value of waste

Every organic gardener should make compost – green waste rotted into a nutritious, soil-like material. Choose a compost bin carefully, the larger the bin, the more heat the compost will generate and the faster you'll make compost. A bin should be around 1m (3ft) square, well ventilated with good air circulation and drainage and must have a cover to keep rain out.

Garden clippings and organic household waste are the principal ingredients of a good compost mix. Never include anything that will attract vermin. To keep the composting going add an activator every couple of weeks – urine or chicken manure help speed composting, or add fish, blood and bonemeal or seaweed. Mix your compost around once a week until it is 'cooked'. It can take between three and six months to turn waste into good compost, depending on the contents and the time of year. If you need a helping hand to begin with, there is plenty of organic compost and manure available on the market.

For a small household and garden a worm bin is ideal. Wormeries come in kit form containing a bin and the worms – you just provide the waste vegetable matter, which the worms transform into very rich compost.

Nutritious cover crops

A green manure is a crop that is sown to be cut and incorporated into the soil for nutrition. The crop is usually killed off by frost and can then be either hoed or dug in. A broad range of plants can be used as green manure including: the green manure lupin *Lupinus angustifolius*, winter tares (*Vicia* spp.), buckwheat *Fagopyrum esculentum* and poached egg plant *Limnanthes douglasii*.

Controlling pests

It is in dealing with pests that organic gardeners exhibit real cunning, calling on a range of options from erecting barricades to calling in biological controls. Some of the simplest methods are the most effective. Erecting barriers works well against birds, rabbits, flea beetles, carrot flies, cutworms and other grubs – nets, meshes, fleeces and plastic sheets can all be called into action. Wire cages around soft fruit bushes stop the birds getting to them.

Different pests need different approaches. Common preventative measures favoured by organic gardeners against cabbage root flies include sealing off cabbage stems with cardboard, roof felt or old carpet. Laying a length of carpet over the lawn at night brings leather jackets and other lawn pests to the surface where they can be disposed of; encircling plants with egg shells, wood ash and sand to discourage slugs are other simple but effective controls. Or you simply locate the pests, pick them off the soil or the plants then drown them and dispose of them on your compost heap.

All types of traps can be laid. Orange halves, saucers of beer, bran or milk will all appeal to slugs. Wasps can wreak havoc with fruit, and can be trapped with jam jars filled with sugary liquid and covered with paper – pierced for access to let them in but not out! Straw-filled flower pots on sticks are popular with earwigs. Birds can be deterred with fine cotton threads woven around tempting plants, or with a bird scarer constructed from flapping bags, metal discs or ribbons – although these have to be regularly switched to be effective as the birds rapidly become accustomed to them. Sticky bands on tree trunks can stop crawling pests, but don't affect predators that usually fly.

Actively encourage natural predators into your garden: hoverflies, ladybirds, lacewings and assorted beetles are all especially effective aphid and slug controllers. Open-centred flowers attract hoverflies and, if you build shelters made from hollow stems or plant some evergreen shrubs, you can give lacewings a place to overwinter. Companion planting is another useful strategy, attracting predators into the garden or deterring pests such as carrot fly that hunt by smell.

Biological control methods – which means using a natural predator to deal with a pest – have made huge advances over the last twenty years and many are readily available commercially, usually by mail order (*see Organic Directory*). There are biological systems to help you control many pests, from vine weevil to red spider mite. Parasitic wasps *Encarsia formosa* will munch on whitefly and destroy cabbage caterpillars. The predatory mite *Phytoseilus* will digest the red spider mite. Most forms of biological control are more suitable for use in greenhouses, but if you have a problem with slugs, for example, you can buy *Phasmarhabditis* and introduce them into the soil to kill slugs. Applied early in the season they can be very effective in minimizing slug damage.

Soil

Soil is graded according to its clay, silt and sand content. The size and proportion of these mineral particles affect the behaviour of the soil. Loam soils have the perfect combination of mineral particle sizes with around 10–25 per cent clay – a mix that offers high fertility with good drainage and water retention. All soils can be improved with compost, manure and lime.

Clay soil
- Heavy, slow-draining soil, often with high nutrient content. Easily damaged and compacted soil structure
- Slow to warm in spring

Sandy soil
- Light, dry, free-draining soil, easy to work but not very fertile. Can be improved by incorporating organic matter and feeding and irrigating frequently
- Warms up quickly in spring

Chalk soil
- Shallow and stony, chalk is moderately fertile and free draining
- Warms up quickly in spring

Silt
- More fertile and moisture-retentive than sandy soil, but easily damaged structure with compaction
- Warms up quickly in spring

the vegetable garden

The kitchen garden is the one area of organic gardening that has the most immediate and positive pay-off. What could be more satisfying than eating your own, home-grown, pesticide-free fruit and vegetables? Anyone who has eaten organic food can confirm the improvement in flavour. The good news is that growing your own takes the flavour factor a stage further as produce picked fresh from the garden has a unique quality all of its own.

The productive space

Fruit and vegetable crops will prove most rewarding if they are given their own space in which to thrive. They require more nutrient-rich soil than other plants and will tend to starve or suffocate their neighbours in a flowerbed. But do not be misled into thinking that the vegetable garden is a flower-free zone. On the contrary, flowers attract friendly predators to consume the pests that destroy your lovingly tended fruit and vegetables. Hoverflies, which help control aphids, are attracted to flat-headed yellow flowers; nasturtiums (*Tropaeolum* spp.) lure blackfly and woolly aphids away from other crops, while chives *Allium schoenoprasum* help to deter carrot flies. Other useful companion plants include marigolds (*Tagetes* spp.), fennel *Foeniculum vulgare*, the cone flower *Echinacea purpurea* and the California poppy *Eschscholzia californica*. A few tall canes of fragrant sweet peas *Lathyrus odoratus* will add a new dimension to the regimented appearance of the vegetable plot.

Rustic poles set in wigwams for runner beans, lines of pea sticks waiting to provide support, rows of onions drying on the soil, rhubarb forcers, cloches and watering cans are all part of the basic charm of the kitchen garden. If you simply don't have enough space for a plot at home you could contact your local council about renting an allotment. This should produce enough vegetables for a family of four to be all but self-sufficient and rents are often next to nothing per year.

The site

Ideally, a vegetable plot should be situated in a sunny position, if at all possible on a gentle slope so that the soil will heat up faster in the spring. Exposed sites should be screened with hedges or fencing to protect crops. Vegetables do not do well in shade nor under trees. Wherever possible, try to ensure that your fruit and vegetables are planted close to a water supply as this will save you effort in the long run.

User-friendly beds

A well-designed vegetable garden is easy to work. Long thin beds, no wider than about 2m (6½ft), are favoured. These proportions make beds easy to work from either side without trampling on the soil, which can damage its structure and fertility. Also plan your space so that it is easy to follow a four-year crop rotation, growing different families of crops in successive positions to avoid a build-up of soil-borne pests and diseases and ensure maximum fertility (*see page 161*). Ideally, plants should sit in rows running north–south as this allows them to receive equal levels of light.

Vegetables such as broccoli, cauliflower and beet prefer to grow in a neutral to slightly alkaline soil, while fruits like strawberries and raspberries tend to prefer the soil neutral to slightly acid. It is worth checking what each plant prefers as rules are not hard and fast – potatoes, for instance, relish the slightly acid soil favoured by soft fruit.

If your ground is very infertile, the solution could be to construct a raised bed and work on improving the fertility within it. Raised beds are relatively simple to build and can be made from stone, brick or timber. Recycled railway sleepers make construction very simple, but they can leach toxic chemicals. Raised beds should be built to a height of 60–75cm (24–30in) and the bottom third should be filled with coarse drainage material – broken bricks and stone – before the topsoil is added. You can grow plants with different soil requirements in the same bed by sectioning off different areas with plastic sheeting during construction.

Selecting for taste

The fun bit for the gardener in all this preparation is planning what produce to grow. When planning your crops be aware of the fruit and vegetables that grow well in your locality. Your garden will be more productive if you select crops that suit your soil and climate. Get hold of some good organic seed catalogues and see what takes your fancy, but try not to get carried away. Aim initially to grow only the family's favourite fruit and vegetables as there is nothing worse than massive crops of something you like to eat only a few times a year.

Draw a plan of what you intend to grow where and remember that you can always put a fast-growing crop such as rocket or lettuce between a slow-growing crop like sweetcorn. This is called intercropping and allows you to harvest the first fast-growing crop before the slower-growing one requires the space. It also means that the ground is always well covered so there is less room for weeds to move in. Some vegetable crops need to be planted once a year and others need to be continually resown. The classic beginner's mistake is to sow two hundred lettuce seeds all at the same time!

Set aside an area of your vegetable plot for a seed bed. This is a section used for protecting and nurturing young crops, a space where you must focus more of your limited time and attention. It allows you to control and extend your harvesting by transplanting young plants at regular intervals to their final positions – transplanting checks growth for a few days and allows plant maturity to be graded to suit. Seed beds can contain anything from brassicas to biennials, which need transplanting, or cuttings slowly growing on.

Fruit is incredibly easy to grow and, compared with vegetables, the rewards from a few plants can be staggering. One or two redcurrant and blackcurrant bushes can provide masses of fruit that is blessedly easy to freeze. Apples, plums and pears require merely an annual prune.

Keep your crops plan for posterity and record how much success you have with which varieties. It will help you make a more educated selection the following year.

Rotation

Gardeners need to be aware of the principles of crop rotation. Vegetables fit into nine major family groups and closely related vegetables are susceptible to the same sets of problems. If you grow the same vegetable, or a related vegetable, in the same spot every year you are very likely to build up associated pests and diseases and your crops will be ruined.

There are four main rotation groups (*see box, right*) so you need to draw up a list of what you are growing, put them in their rotation groups and plant your vegetable garden accordingly. Wait at least three to four years between planting related crops. Keep your plan and try to record how each crop performed – this will help you develop a more productive vegetable garden long term.

Sowing

Hardy vegetables, such as potatoes, parsnips, onions and spinach, that can withstand the cold, are generally sown straight into the soil when it has warmed up to 6°C/43°F. You don't have to use a special soil thermometer to determine when you can plant – if the grass has started to grow the soil temperature is suitable for sowing.

Four-year crop rotation
Growing different families of crops in successive positions over four years helps avoid a build-up of soil-borne pests and diseases.

1 – Legumes and pods
Broad beans ● French beans ● Runner beans ● Okra ● Peas

2 – Alliums
Garlic ● Leeks ● Bulb onions ● Spring onions ● Shallots ● Welsh onions

3 – Solanaceous, tuberous and root crops
Aubergines ● Beetroot ● Carrots ● Celery ● Celeriac ● Parsnips ● Potatoes ● Sweet potatoes ● Sweet peppers ● Tomatoes

4 – Brassicas
Brussel sprouts ● Broccoli ● Cabbage ● Cauliflower ● Kale ● Kohlrabi ● Pak choi ● Radishes ● Swede ● Turnips

Some like it hot

Tender plants, such as basil or tomatoes, cannot withstand frost and will at best tolerate cool weather. They are best started off indoors, sowing the seeds in pots or trays and then planting them out when things have hotted up outside. Courgettes, runner and French beans are also tender plants, but they can be sown directly into the soil once it has reached 12°C/54°F. A little protection early in the season with cloches or fleece will help get them off to a good start.

Seed beds

When you are ready to sow your seeds make sure that your prepared soil has a fine crumbly surface. Rake it level to get rid of any clods of earth and to remove any stones. Heavy soil must never be dug when it is wet as this can cause serious structural damage.

Allow yourself time to plant seeds with love and care or you will have to put up with a wobbly plant line or poor spacing for the rest of the year. A good start will help give you good, long-term results. Sow seeds in straight drills, to the required depth, using a line. This simple device is just a length of string with wooden pegs at each end and it allows you to mark out your rows for precision planting. Once the seeds are sown, water until the soil is moist, but use a fine spray as you do not want to disturb the precious seeds. Do check instructions on the seed packet before you sow as different seeds have different requirements – some even do best if soaked in water for 24 hours prior to sowing. Keep the soil moist if the weather isn't doing the work for you. Thin the seedlings as they come through but try to do this when the soil is damp or you could damage the root systems of the remaining plants.

Keep a look out for pests at this stage. If birds are a problem try threading cotton around a network of sticks or simply use a net tunnel – they are easy to buy or make. You may need to cover crops with cloches or plastic tunnels or spread gritty barriers around them to protect them from slugs or pests that fly.

Keep well watered

Any crop will suffer if it doesn't get enough water so you must take steps to ensure you can give your plants what they need. Compost, leaf mould or any organic matter incorporated into the soil will help it to retain moisture. Mulching is very effective, but make a slight depression around the plants to encourage rainwater to run on to the plants and not away from them. Weeds must also be kept in check as they will take much-needed moisture, as well as nutrients, from the soil and compete with your crop.

Food supplements

Hungry plants can make extra demands on your lovingly prepared and nutrient-rich soil. As they guzzle up the goodness the soil may require an extra feed in the form of an organic fertilizer. Fertilizers are rated according to their nitrogen (N), phosphorous (P) and potassium (K) content. Nitrogen stimulates growth and leaves, phosphorous benefits the roots and potassium boosts disease resistance and fruiting; choose appropriately to suit your plants' particular requirements. Apart from compost and manure, organic fertilizers come in various other forms – from pelleted chicken manure (be very careful to ensure it is genuine organic waste) to liquid feeds such as comfrey *Symphytum officinale* or stinging nettle *Urtica dioica* (*see page 173*).

But do take care not to overfeed your soil; too much fertilizer can result in lush, sappy plant growth, which merely succeeds in attracting pests and diseases. A well-prepared soil that contains plenty of good organic compost should not require additional fertilizer.

Gardeners need to be particularly alert to any signs of plant ill health. A yellowing leaf or two, or some nibbled greenery might not seem much of a problem initially, but ignore the early warnings and you may have to write off your entire crop. Pick off infected or pest-ridden leaves and burn or bury them good and deep. Sterilize any secateurs, knives or saws that come into contact with infected material. Don't forget to give children a tiny space of their own in your kitchen garden. As a child, there is nothing more likely to foster a future love of gardening than being given your own little patch for growing things. Start them off with either extra tasty or impressively sized fruits or flowers. Strawberries, pumpkins, tomatoes and sunflowers *Helianthus annuum* are especially rewarding for little ones. Children always love to help with the watering and harvesting – even if they sometimes refuse to eat the end results!

Yields

The yields from your crops can be unpredictable and will depend very much on the individual growing conditions of your vegetable patch – the fertility of the soil, at what stage the crop is harvested, any pest and disease problems, unseasonal weather and the amount of watering your plants receive. With crops such as cabbage and cauliflower, essentially you harvest what you plant. For plants such as tomatoes and courgettes, the success of the yield is determined by the weight of the harvested crop. Courgettes are an example of a crop where regular and careful harvesting can improve the final yield.

the flower garden

Although people tend to associate organic gardening with the cultivation of fruit and vegetables, they somehow do not expect the same enthusiasm to be thrown into flower cultivation. The fact is that some of the loveliest flower gardens are organic and this is because a good organic flower garden is balanced and structured in design and rich in content.

Natural environment

The key to good organic flower gardening is twofold: soil conditioning (*see page 149*) and good plant husbandry. You must allow your choice of plants to be dictated by your local climate and soil. No matter how much you prize certain plants, if they are not suited to your environment then it is pointless to try to grow them. Moreover, defying the natural limitations of your environment produces an unreal effect. Gardens that struggle to combine the most unlikely mix of plants look unreal and unnatural.

You should aim to achieve a balanced and harmonious planting scheme containing year-round interest. Later-flowering plants, autumn berries, the water feature, the hedge screens and the structural evergreen feature all provide late-season interest and also sustain wildlife, providing food and shelter.

In determining a balanced planting scheme first look at the structure of your flower garden. Draw a plan marking out key plants and highlight the aspect of each bed. Is it south or north facing? Is it open to day-long sunshine or dappled by light shade? When you know the answers, you can choose your plants to suit each area accordingly.

Backbone plants

Shrubs, trees and hedges form the backbone of any planting scheme. Every garden should contain at least one tree, but it must be appropriate to the size of the garden. Weeping willows *Salix babylonica* or oaks (*Quercus* spp.) are not suitable for the average suburban garden. Fruit trees are good value for the organic gardener with blossom in spring and fruit in the autumn. The best ornamental trees such as hawthorn (*Craetagus* spp.) boast glorious blossom in spring, good autumn colour and bright berries.

Good hedging is like a backdrop to the garden, it highlights layout and structure. Solid blocks of hedging that draw the eye do not serve any purpose. Try to steer clear of the more obvious hedging plants such as privet (*Ligustrum* spp.), and avoid using conifers, which are high maintenance in terms of cutting, drain the soil of nutrients and can easily become an overdominant, unnatural feature. The native yew *Taxus baccata* or beech *Fagus sylvatica* make good formal hedges, but for a natural look that shelters a wide diversity of wildlife opt for native hedgerow plants with a mix of hawthorn *Craetagus monocarpa*, holly *Ilex aquifolium*, blackthorn *Prunus spinosa* and rose (*Rosa* spp.). Don't forget the low-screening potential of box (*Buxus* spp.)*,* lavender (*Lavandula* spp.) and rosemary *Rosmarinus officinalis*, which can add dignity and charm to even a frozen vegetable patch in the depths of winter.

Shrubs for all seasons

Shrubs should offer a good mix of flowering seasons and ideally provide an element of evergreen interest in the garden. *Eleagnus* (*Eleagnus* spp.) is a tough and attractive evergreen, carrying tiny barely visible flowers that perfume the air. Choisya *Choisya ternata* is a glossy evergreen with fragrant spring flowers that attract insects. There are evergreen and deciduous viburnums that will flower at times throughout the year, including *Viburnum bodnantense* 'Dawn' which has superbly fragrant flowers on bare boughs in early winter.

Herbs such as rosemary *Rosmarinus officinalis* and bay *Laurus nobilis* will grow very large in sheltered sunny spots. Equally, lavender and cotton lavender (*Santolina* spp.) will provide some permanent structure at the front of the border. Euphorbias (*Euphorbia* spp.) have poisonous sap but offer good, dense evergreen cover in the border – there are a number of spectacular varieties to suit a wide range of situations.

Roses are great garden favourites and attract many insects, but they can be highly susceptible to pests and diseases. Avoid delicate strains, consult the growers and take advice about varieties of rose with good resistance to mildew or rust. Apply a good compost mulch or manure every autumn.

Use companion planting to try and distract pests. If you have a problem with whitefly you could try growing hops *Humulus lupus* so as to attract ladybirds. If aphids are abundant try planting chives *Allium schoenoprasum*, which they dislike, or sacrifice nasturtiums *Tropaeolum majus*, which they love.

Cover-ups

Ideally, attractive climbing plants should be planted against walls, fences and posts or to scramble over unsightly buildings or through shrubs to give an extended flowering season. There are plants to suit every aspect. Common favourite climbers are clematis (*Clematis* spp.), passion flower *Passiflora incarnata*, honeysuckle (*Lonicera* spp.), wisteria *(Wisteria* spp.), vines (*Vitis* spp.) and jasmine *Jasminum officinale*.

Divide and rule

Herbaceous perennials are those plants that die back every autumn when the frosts come. These will give the garden its annual change of emphasis and height. This group includes such favourites as windflowers (*Anemone* spp.), cone flowers (*Echinacea* spp.) and peonies (*Paeonia* spp.), day lilies (*Hemerocallis* spp.), delphiniums (*Delphinium* spp.), catmint *Nepeta mussinii* and sedum (*Sedum* spp.). Most of these plants require very little in the way of attention; as long as you condition the soil, tidy up in autumn and lift and divide your clumps every few years in the spring, they will perform beautifully with no fuss.

Dividing plants is straightforward, insert two garden forks back to back In the middle of a clump in autumn, then lever them gently apart, removing one clump to replant and refirming the soil round the existing plant.

Year on year

Annuals grow, flower and die back every year from seed. Try to grow varieties that will seed themselves freely such as California poppy *Eschscholzia californica*, love-in-a-mist *Nigella damascena* and nasturtiums *Tropaeolum majus*. Biennials grow from seed one year, and flower and die the following year. Foxgloves (*Digitalis* spp.) are the best known of these but the group includes Canterbury bells *Campanula persicifolia*, sweet Williams *Dianthus barbatus*, hollyhocks *Althea rosea* and wallflowers *Erysimum cheiranthus*. If the situation suits them they will start self-seeding and will pop up all over the garden.

Bulbs

Bulbs can be grown in borders as well as being naturalized in grass. Choose varieties that will keep on flowering year after year – some of the more exotic tulip strains are stunning, but they will flower only once. Choose strong, disease-resistant varieties and try to ensure you have something flowering throughout the year. Snowdrops *Galanthus nivalis* are often the first flower to mark the start of the new growing season, these are best bought just after they have flowered. Daffodils (*Narcissus* spp.) and fritillaries (*Fritillaria* spp.) will naturalize in the grass. If you want to avoid regimental groupings throw handfuls of the bulbs around and then plant them where they fall. Don't cut the leaves back after flowering until they have naturally started to wither – cutting back too early reduces the flowering in future seasons. In summer there are lilies (*Lilium* spp.) and alliums (*Allium* spp.), and in autumn cyclamen (*Cyclamen coum* spp.) nerine (*Nerine* spp.) and the beautiful, but poisonous, autumn crocus (*Colchicum* spp.).

grow your own

Whispering grass

Ornamental grasses are another group of plants that should not be overlooked in your planting scheme. Examples range from tall rangy specimens to small front-of-the-border wisps. They bring a wonderful movement to the garden and birds love them – raiding them constantly for nest material. Look out for varieties such as *Stipa gigantea*, which has beautiful tall seed heads, *Carex comans,* which is an evergreen mop of bronze leaves, or the outsize *Miscanthus sacchariflorus*.

Water elements

Water features need sympathetic planting to look good and to support pond life. Don't site ponds too close to trees, or leaf fall will encourage the growth of algae and suffocate everything. Don't put anything into a newly filled pond for at least a week, this allows the water to warm up and the chlorine to filter away. If you want to give the eco-system a head start take a bucketful of water and mud from a local pond and deposit it in your water feature. You will also require oxygenating plants to aerate the water, prevent algae from taking over and to provide shelter for pond life. Depending on your personal choice you can add water lilies (*Nymphaea* spp.), iris (*Iris* spp.) and kingcups *Caltha palustris* or angel's fishing rod *Dierama pulcherrimum* in boggy ground alongside.

the herb garden

Herbs are among the most rewarding plants to grow. A meal can be completely transformed with the addition of a few pungent leaves, freshly picked, chopped and in a dish on the table within minutes. Their scented flowers and leaves excite the senses and inspire a feeling of well-being, while attracting many beneficial insects to your garden.

Instinctive appeal

Herbs are not by nature showy plants, yet they quietly command attention. Designated herb beds are usually the most tranquil areas of any garden – a place where you want to stop, sit and breathe deeply. This should not be surprising, as herbs are the most powerful plants in horticulture. Alternative therapies such as homeopathy and herbalism have long recognized their power, and scientists are now conducting serious research into the properties of herbs. Foxglove, or digitalis, was the basis for the powerful drug digitoxin used for treating heart failure; it has recently been discovered that St John's wort *Hypericum perforatum* can help alleviate certain forms of depression, and sage *Salvia officinalis* may yet help treat Alzheimer's disease. However, herbs should be used under guidance from a qualified herbal practitioner. They are powerful plants and must be treated with caution – even the common culinary sage can prove toxic if drunk too often as a tea.

Low maintenance

A group of perennial herbs require very little maintenance save a bit of annual pruning and harvesting. Most will perform quite well in pots and are much more appealing and eco-friendly than a succession of bedding plants. Mint (*Mentha* spp.) should always be grown in a pot as its roots can otherwise rapidly spread and become a nuisance.

Quite apart from their good looks and culinary lure, herbs have the added bonus of being very resistant to pests and diseases. They are often used in vegetable gardens as companion plants, notably chives *Allium schoenoprasum*, parsley *Petroselinum crispum*, thyme (*Thymus* spp.) and hyssop *Hyssopus officinalis*. The fragrance of some herbs effectively acts as an insect repellent; among those reputed to discourage pests and diseases are chives *Allium schoenoprasum* and garlic *Allium sativum*.

Lore and order

Traditionally, herb gardens were planted in formal geometric patterns, close to the kitchen for easy accessibility. Such planting schemes can contain medicinal, aromatic or culinary herbs or a generous mix of varieties. Many herbs rank as some of our best-loved plants. Think of fragrant lavender (*Lavandula* spp.), lemon balm *Melissa officinalis*, camomile *Chamaemelum nobile*, beautiful fennel *Foeniculum vulgare*, bergamot *Monarda didymus* and scented juniper *Juniperus communis*. Favoured medicinal herbs include comfrey *Symphytum officinale*, feverfew *Tanacetum parthenium*, heartsease *Viola tricolor*, peppermint *Mentha piperita* and pot marigold *Calendula officinalis*. Designated herb gardens are very attractive, but it is perfectly possible to use herbs throughout the garden. Herbs such as clipped lavender and rosemary make perfect edging for a vegetable or flowerbed and as you brush against them their intense perfumes will please you – and a variety of beneficial insects – all summer long.

Warm and dry

A site for growing herbs must be dry and sunny. Most culinary herbs originate in the Mediterranean so they will not thrive in rich soil, instead preferring sandy, free-draining ground. These plants like warmth and particularly enjoy close proximity to stone, brick and gravel, which bounces the heat back at them.

Perfumed steps

Camomile lawns release a wonderful fragrance when walked upon, but they are much harder to establish and maintain than a grass lawn. Good, low-growing varieties to choose from include *Chamaemelum nobile* 'Flore Pleno' or 'Treneague'. A camomile lawn should be laid on foundations of 8cm (3in) hardcore, 8cm (3in) gravel and 15cm (6in) topsoil. Plants should be 10–15cm (4–6in) apart, and you must keep off the area for at least twelve weeks. Then trim the plants regularly to prevent them going straggly.

Harvest festival

Pick and use fresh herbs freely, and dry some for the winter. The faster they are dried, the more essential oils and flavour they will retain. Lay them out on well-ventilated racks covered in muslin and store them in a dark, airy place such as an airing cupboard for several days, turning them once or twice. Drying times vary; when dried, herbs should feel brittle but not too crumbly. Store them in screw-top jars away from direct sunlight.

Freezing is an excellent way to preserve herbs. Place them in labelled bags, but give them space as they can be easily damaged. You can also freeze some herbs in ice cubes for summer drinks – borage *Borago officinalis* flowers and mint leaves are perfect mixers.

Starting with seed

Site preparation, as for any other form of organic gardening, is crucial. Herbs are happiest in a fairly neutral soil with a pH balance of between 6.5 and 7.5. Most herbs can be sown directly into the garden in mid- to late spring – with the exception of basil and sweet marjoram. Basil *Ocimum basilicum* seedlings tend to rot in the damp northern climate and sweet marjoram *Origanum hortensis* seeds are so small they are better started off in a pot. Sow the seeds thinly and thin out to two or three per 2.5cm (1in). If you start seeds off indoors harden them off for a few days by taking them in and out during the day before planting them in their final positions outside.

Layering

Woody herbs such as thyme and sage can easily be increased by layering. Bring a healthy stem down to the soil in spring and peg it into the ground so that the growing tip is vertical. The stem will form new roots. The following autumn liberate the plant from its parent, but let it remain where it has rooted for another year before transplanting.

Cuttings

Cuttings are an effective way of multiplying your stock. There are four different types of cuttings - softwood, semi-hardwood or greenwood, hardwood and root. Always use a clean sharp knife to take cuttings.

Cutting type	Softwood cuttings	Semi hardwood or greenwood cuttings	Hardwood cuttings	Root cuttings
Time of year	Spring	Mid-summer to mid-autumn	Mid–late autumn	Spring or autumn
Method	Cut fresh, young growth from the plant and trim cleanly before a node (leaf joint). Remove leaves from the bottom third of the cutting.	Cut fresh, young growth from the plant and trim cleanly before a node (leaf joint). Remove leaves from the bottom third of the cutting.	Cut fresh, young growth from the plant and trim cleanly before a node (leaf joint). Remove leaves from the bottom third of the cutting.	Cut a 4–8cm (2–3in) length of root with a growing bud where visible and plant the cutting vertically. Do not water until top growth appears.
Growing medium	50% bark, 50% organic potting compost.	Equal mix of grit, organic potting compost and bark.	Equal parts grit, organic potting compost and bark.	50% bark, 50% organic potting compost.
Care	Put the cuttings in a propagator, heated or unheated, or you can use a plastic bag if you regularly turn it inside out to prevent moisture build up, but keep the plastic away from the cutting leaves. Spray the plants daily.	These should be kept in a cold greenhouse or cold frame and should not be over watered. Plants should be hardened off in the spring.	Winter in a cold frame, greenhouse or conservatory.	Plant root cuttings vertically, cover and label. Harden off the cuttings when rooted and plant out in the spring.
Time to Root	Two to four weeks.	Four to six weeks.	Up to one year.	Two to three weeks.
Suitable plants	Lavender, marjoram, mint, rosemary, rue, sage, tarragon, thyme.	Shrubby herbs, such as elder, juniper, lavender, myrtle, rosemary and thyme.	Buddleja, box, honeysuckle, rose.	This method is used for plants with creeping root systems such as chamomile, comfrey, horseradish, lemon balm and mint.

grow your own

patios
and pots

If the garden is the big picture, your terrace or patio is the close-up. Left bare it can look drab and uninviting, but add some colour, texture and structure with interesting pots and plants and the space is transformed. Even working in this smallest of spaces the organic gardener can make a mark.

Pocket gardening

Aim to create an area that will be fruitful and fragrant as well as looking good. If this is all the space you have, grow some favourite annual herbs or a good crop of tomatoes and some interesting salad leaves, as well as favourite flowers. Herbs will enjoy basking in warmth on a sunny patio and lavender (*Lavandula* spp.) and bay *Laurus nobilis* grow well in pots and can be clipped into formal shapes, as can box (*Buxus* spp.), to provide some year-round structural interest. Ornamental grasses will shiver in the wind and introduce height and movement.

Long-term style

Apart from edible plants and herbs, long-term plantings are most suitable for an organic garden patio. Choose permanent trees and shrubs, with perhaps a climber or two, and freshen up your display by underplanting with bulbs. Place miniature daffodils *Narcissus* 'Tête-à-Tête' or iris *Iris reticulata* around a container-planted fruit tree, for example, and you will have a glorious seasonal show.

Containers also give you the opportunity to grow plants that would not be suited to your garden soil – azaleas (*Azalea* spp.) and heathers (*Erica* spp.) for example will thrive in pots of ericaceous compost.

Try to use the largest containers your space will permit, at least 25 x 25cm (10 x 10in). Ensure you have good drainage at the bottom of the pot, put some crocks or some gravel at the base and if you worry about soil leaching through then a piece of sacking or muslin will serve as a barrier. Wherever possible sit the container in a water-retaining tray over the hottest months of the year. Gravel, stones, shell, glass beads and china fragments can all be used as a decorative mulch – they look good, help prevent the sun from baking the surface of the soil and discourage weeds.

There are plenty of organic composts suitable for container gardening, or you can make your own. A growing medium must be water retentive and well aerated, with a structure that can withstand heavy watering. Garden soil is not a suitable medium for container gardening as it compacts too readily and becomes waterlogged and airless. It should only be used, mixed with garden compost, for permanent plantings such as fruit trees and woody shrubs. A good blend for other container planting is two parts matured garden compost, one part loam and one part bark. To every 10 litres (2 gallons) add 25g (1oz) hoof and horn, 25g (1oz) seaweed meal and 20g (¾oz) bonemeal.

Different mixes suit different plant requirements – use well-rotted leaf mould alone or a mix of leaf mould, sterilized soil and sand for sowing seeds. Nutrient-rich worm compost is an ideal feed for hungry hanging baskets or for giving containers a boost. Never line a hanging basket with moss, instead use hay and compressed paper, or cocoa moss or cocoa fibre liners.

Feeding up

You can make your own liquid fertilizer from comfrey *Symphytum officinale* or nettles *Urtica dioica*. Pack leaves into a bucket or barrel, cover with water and leave for two or three weeks. The result is a very dark and smelly soup, which should be watered down to a pale yellow before use.

Maintenance

Container-grown plants need regular watering and feeding as they are totally dependent on the gardener, rather than being able to get the nutrition they need from a living garden soil. Perennial plantings also need to be lifted and divided every year or two. They may require top-dressing – replacing the top layer of the soil with new compost and fertilizer, or they may need to be moved to a larger pot if they become root bound.

paths, paving and decking

When you are following organic principles don't overlook the hard landscaping of your garden. While at present there are no hard-and-fast rules regarding the use of many landscaping materials, you should follow organic principles and try to recycle as much as possible. Materials should be durable and locally sourced as the environmental impact is less if materials have not been transported across the country.

Second-hand stone

Natural landscaping materials such as flagstones, bricks, slate and gravel all look good, but can be expensive and have to be quarried. Therefore a good starting point for any landscaping project is a reclamation centre. Try to be flexible about your scheme – a combination of stone, slate, brick and gravel can make a stunning terrace. Someone else's discarded piece of statuary or metal arch could make a focal point in the garden. Landscaping projects can be costly, but if you gather discarded bricks from the skip of a sympathetic builder, or a piece of driftwood from the beach, you can create a feature for next to nothing.

Natural lifespan

It is in the use of timber in the garden that organic gardeners should be most cautious. It is crucial that wood comes from sustainable sources; wherever possible try to use reliable local suppliers and while no hard-line organic standards exist relating to wood preservatives there are some best practice guidelines to follow.

Wood preservatives are by their nature persistent toxic products used to prevent rot and decay by bacterial and fungicidal agents. Wood decays fastest where soil and air meet, such as at the base of a fence post. If posts are concreted in or slipped into metal shoes, preservatives are unnecessary. Compost boxes and timber for bed and lawn edging is often sold treated, but need not be. Wood can last many years without preservatives; it is better to replace it at intervals rather than use chemical preservatives.

Wood varies in durability so try to select timber best suited to its purpose. Oak, western red cedar and sweet chestnut should last around twenty years in contact with the ground, pine around five years and larch about ten years, all without any preservatives. Well-seasoned wood is more likely to be most resistant to decay.

Sustainable sources

Most timber and fencing sold for external use is almost
certainly to be sold pretreated. Take great care when opting
for decking to find a company that uses sustainable,
untreated wood. Properly laid decking doesn't have to be
doused in chemicals to last. Railway sleepers are recycled,
but they also leach toxic tar into the environment so you
have to weigh the advantages against the disadvantages.

Do-it-yourself

There are plenty of alternatives to treated fence panels.
Hazel or willow hurdles are very attractive, made from
coppiced wood farmed for the purpose, and can be ordered
to size. Erect a bamboo screen, plant a native hedge or
make rustic garden gates – surprisingly easy to make and a
charming, individual alternative to anything you could buy.

Paths and paving

The first question to ask is 'Do I need it?' It may be more
practical to lay a few stepping stones into grass, for
example, rather than introducing a solid path. While most
paths need to be wide enough to accommodate a wheelbarrow, check if this is necessary or can you get away
with a narrow walkway? One of the principles of organic
gardening is to keep external inputs to a minimum so never
introduce more materials from outside your garden than are
strictly necessary.

The simple rule in landscaping is to try to recycle and be as
natural as possible. There are no rules to say don't lay a
brick path on a bed of concrete, but it would be gentler to
mortar the edges and lay the rest on a bed of sharp sand.
By brushing a dry mortar and sand mix between the bricks
you can keep unnecessary weeding to a minimum.

organic directory

This directory is an introductory selection of organizations, useful contacts and nationwide suppliers of organic products. The directory is grouped according to the chapters in the book and listings are generally arranged alphabetically within sections.

Organizations

The Soil Association

Bristol House, 40–56 Victoria Street,
Bristol BS1 6BY
Tel: 0117 929 0661
Fax: 0117 925 2504
E: info@soilassociation.org
W: www.soilassociation.org

The UK's leading group, working to
promote the benefits of organic food,
farming and sustainable forestry to
human health, animal welfare and the
environment. It publishes the *Soil
Association Directory* and its website
features a searchable database of
organic producers, suppliers and
organizations throughout the UK.

Biodynamic Agricultural
Association (BDAA)

Painswick Inn, Stroud,
Gloucester GL5 1QG
Tel/Fax: 01453 759501
E: bdaa@biodynamic.freeserve.co.uk
W: www.anth.org.uk/biodynamic/

Part of a worldwide movement
promoting the biodynamic approach to
agriculture arising from Rudolf Steiner's
spiritual scientific research.

Centre for Alternative Technology

Machynlleth, Powys SY20 9AZ
Tel: 01654 702400
Fax: 01654 702782
E: info@cat.org.uk
W: www.cat.org.uk

Internationally renowned display
and education centre, promoting
technologies that sustain rather
than damage the environment.

Friends of the Earth

26–28 Underwood Street,
London N1 7QJ
Tel: 020 7490 1555
Fax: 020 7490 0881
E: info@foe.co.uk
W: www.foe.co.uk

A leading UK pressure group that
campaigns on a wide range of local,
national and international
environmental issues.

The Genetics Forum

94 White Lion Street,
London N1 9PF
Tel: 020 7837 9229
Fax: 020 7837 1141
E: geneticsforum@gn.apc.org
W: www.geneticsforum.org.uk

Public interest group, devoted to
research and campaigns on genetic
engineering from a social, ethical and
environmental perspective.

The Green Network

9 Clairmont Road, Lexden,
Colchester, Essex CO3 5BE
Tel: 01206 546902
Fax: 01206 766005

National network made up of
individuals, organizations and
businesses promoting positive
action for the environment.

Greenpeace

Canonbury Villas,
London N1 2PN
Tel: 020 7865 8100
Fax: 020 7865 8200
E: info@uk.greenpeace.org
W: www.greenpeace.org.uk

Global environmental campaigning
organization. Includes action against
genetically modified foods.

Henry Doubleday Research
Association (HDRA)

Ryton Organic Gardens, Ryton-on-
Dunsmore, Coventry CV8 3LG

Tel: 024 7630 3517
Fax: 024 7663 9229
E: enquiry@hdra.org.uk
W: www.hdra.org.uk

Vast organization that researches,
advises and provides information on
organic gardening, growing and food.

Pesticide Action Network UK

Eurolink Centre, 49 Effra Road,
London SW2 1BZ
Tel: 020 7274 8895
Fax: 020 7274 9084
E: admin@pan-uk.org
W: www.pan-uk.org

PAN UK represents consumers and
campaigns to promote alternatives to
pesticide use and to stop hazardous
exports.

Women's Environmental Network

P. O. Box 30626, London E1 1TZ
Tel: 020 7481 9004
Fax: 020 7481 9144
E: info@wen.org.uk
W: www.wen.org.uk

WEN aims to educate, empower and
inform on matters related to women
and the environment. Campaigns

include encouraging local food growing projects, waste minimization, health and the environment, sanitary protection and nappies.

Worldwide Fund for Nature UK
Panda House, Weyside Park,
Godalming, Surrey GU7 1XR
Tel: 01483 426444
Fax: 01483 426409
E: wwf-uk-supportercare@wwf.org.uk
W: www.wwf-uk.org

Well-known non-governmental organization; campaigns on local, national and international levels for conservation of the environment and plants, animals and people within it.

Eating and Drinking

Certification/Organizations:
Independent UK Register of Organic Food Standards (UKROFS)
Room 320C, c/o Ministry of Agriculture, Fisheries and Food, Nobel House, 17 Smith Square, London SW1P 3JR
Tel: 020 7238 5915
Fax: 020 7238 6148

Government body that sets basic standards of organic produce.

Approves and supervises the other certification bodies.

Soil Association Certification Ltd
Bristol House, 40–56 Victoria Street,
Bristol BS1 6BY
Tel: 0117 914 2405
Fax: 0117 925 2504
E: cert@soilassociation.org
W: www.soilassociation.org

The largest of UK certification bodies, currently inspects and certifies over 70 per cent of UK-licensed organic producers and processors.

Organic Farmers and Growers Ltd
The Elin Centre, Lancaster Road,
Shrewsbury SY1 3LE
Tel: 01743 440512
Fax: 01743 461481

Second largest UK organic certification body, licensed to certify organic production, processing and retailing.

Organic Food Federation
Unit 1, Manor Enterprise Centre,
Mowles Manor, Etling Green,
Dereham NR20 3EZ
Tel: 01362 637314
Fax: 01362 637980

Trade federation for the organic food industry, representing importers, manufacturers and producers.

Irish Organic Farmers and Growers Association (IOFGA)
Organic Farm Centre, Harbour Road,
Kilbeggan, Co. West Meath, Ireland
Tel: +353 (0)506 32563
Fax: +353 (0)506 32063
E: iofga@tinet.ie
W: www.homepage.tinet.ie/

Largest organic association in Ireland. It operates an inspection and certification scheme and provides practical information for organic farmers and growers.

Scottish Organic Producers Association (SOPA)
Milton of Cambus Doune,
Perthshire FK16 6HQ
Tel: 01786 841 657
Fax: 01786 842 264
E: contact@sopa.org.uk
W: www.sopa.org.uk

SOPA promotes the interests of organic producers in Scotland under the Scottish Organic label. It operates a verification and certification system for organic produce approved by UKROFS.

International Federation of Organic Agricultural Movements (IFOAM)
Ökozentrum Imsbach, D-66636
Tholey-Theley, Germany
Tel: +49 6853 919890
Fax: +49 6853 919899
E: HeadOffice@ifoam.org
W: www.ifoam.org

The world umbrella organization of the organic agricultural movement. The federation's main function is co-ordinating the network of the organic movement around the world.

Demeter Standards Committee of the Biodynamic Agricultural Association
17 Inverleith Place,
Edinburgh EH3 5QE
Tel: 0131 624 3921
Fax: 0131 476 2996
W: www.anth.org.uk/biodynamic/demeter.htm

Owned and administered by the Biodynamic Agricultural Association, the DEMETER certified trademark guarantees to consumers that produce has been grown according to internationally recognized guidelines for biodynamic agriculture.

Sustain: The alliance for better food and farming

94 White Lion Street, London N1 9PF

Tel: 020 7837 1228

Fax: 020 7837 1141

E: sustain@sustainweb.org

W: www.sustainweb.org

Campaigns for food and agricultural policies and practices that enhance the health and welfare of people and animals and improve the environment.

The Food Commission

94 White Lion Street, London N1 9PF

Tel: 020 7837 2250

Fax: 020 7837 1141

E: foodcomm@compuserve.com

W: www.foodcomm.org.uk

The UK's leading independent watchdog on food issues, campaigning for the right to safer, healthier food.

Buying organic:

Farmers' markets and farm shops:

National Association of Farmers' Markets

South Vaults, Green Park Station, Green Park Road, Bath BA1 1JB

Tel: 01225 787914

Fax: 01225 460840

E: nafm@farmersmarkets.net

W: www.farmersmarkets.net

Association established to develop and support farmers' markets around the UK. See its website for a list of farmers' markets around the country.

Farm Retail Association

The Greenhouse, P. O. Box 575, Southampton SO15 7ZB

Tel/Fax: 023 8036 2150

E: fra@farmshopping.com

W: www.farmshopping.com

Represents over 300 UK farms selling direct through PYO, farm shops, farmers' markets and box schemes.

Home delivery organic supermarkets:

Cooks' Delight

360–364 High Street, Berkhamsted, Herts HP4 1HU

Tel: 01442 863584

Fax: 01442 863702

E: info@organiccooksdelight.co.uk

W: www.organiccooksdelight.co.uk

Organic and biodynamic online and mail-order food shop. Shoppers on the website can filter the catalogue for special diets such as vegan, gluten-

and wheat-free, no-added-sugar and biodynamic products.

The Fresh Food Company

326 Portobello Road, London W10 5RU

Tel: 020 8969 0351

Fax: 020 8964 8050

E: organics@freshfood.co.uk

W: www.freshfood.co.uk

Nationwide service that delivers a huge range of organic food straight to your home. It runs a box scheme for fruit, vegetables, herbs and salads. Also sells organic groceries, wines, beers, breads, eggs, meat, fish, a range of spring waters, cleaning products and personal and babycare products.

Iorganic.com

58–60 Kensington Church Street, London W8 4DB

Tel: 020 7692 4966

Fax: 020 7692 4968

W: www.iorganic.com

Online shop featuring a wide range of fresh fruit and vegetables, general groceries, wine, baby food, vitamins, health and beauty products and household cleaning products.

The Organic Shop Online

The Organic Shop, Freepost, Alderley Edge, Cheshire SK9 7YG

Tel: 0845 674 4000

Fax: 0845 674 1000

E: info@theorganicshop.co.uk

W: www.theorganicshop.co.uk

Online shop featuring a wide range of fresh fruit and vegetables, meat and fish, dairy, bakery, general groceries, wine, beer and spirits, baby food and household cleaning products.

Organics Direct

7 Willow Street, London EC2A 4BH

Tel: 020 7729 2828

Fax: 020 7613 5800

E: info@organicsdirect.co.uk

W: www.organicsdirect.co.uk

Organic vegetarian produce delivered to your home or workplace – anywhere on the UK mainland. Choose from a huge range including fresh fruit and vegetables, dairy produce, hand-made breads, store cupboard items, award-winning wines, beers, baby products, and even organic clothes and nappies.

Simply Organic Food Company Ltd
Unit A62–A64, New Covent Garden
Market, London SW8 5EE
Tel: 0845 1000 444/020 7622 5006
Fax: 020 7622 4447
E: info@simplyorganic.net
W: www.simplyorganic.net

Nationwide daily delivery of vast range
of organic products: fresh produce,
meat, fish, dairy, deli, groceries,
babycare, home and personal care,
clothes, linens, books, wines, beers.

Non-alcoholic drinks:
James White
Whites Fruit Farm, Helminham Road,
Ashbocking, Suffolk IP6 9JS
Tel: 01473 890 111
Fax: 01473 890 001
E: info@jameswhite.co.uk
W: www.jameswhite.co.uk

Range of organic fruit juices, available
for both trade customers and for direct
home delivery throughout the UK.

The Tea and Coffee Plant
170 Portobello Road, London W11 2EB
Tel: 020 7221 8137
E: coffee@pro-net.co.uk
W: www.coffee.uk.com

Freshly roasted organic coffee available
by mail order throughout the UK. Also
supplies organic tea and tea bags.

Alcohol:
Vinceremos Wines and Spirits Ltd
19 New Street, Leeds LS18 4BH
Tel: 0113 205 4545
Fax: 0113 205 4546
E: info@vinceremos.co.uk
W: www.vinceremos.co.uk

Organic and vegetarian wines delivered
to your door. Also supplies organic
beers, ciders, juices and spirits.

Vintage Roots Ltd
Farley Farms, Bridge Farm, Reading
Road, Arborfield RG2 9HT
Tel: 0118 976 1999
Fax: 0118 976 1998
E: info@vintageroots.co.uk
W: www.vintageroots.co.uk

Huge range of organic wines, beers,
spirits, ciders and juices from around
the world, all available by mail order.

Fruit and vegetables:
See also: *Farmers' Markets and Farm
Shops; Meat, Poultry and Fish; Home
Delivery Organic Supermarkets*. See

also *Soil Association Directory* for box
scheme details

**The Organic Marketing
Company Ltd**
Leighton Court, Lower Eggleton,
Ledbury HR8 2UN
Tel: 01531 640819
Fax: 01531 640818
E: mail@organicmarketing.co.uk
W: www.organicmarketing.co.uk

Nationwide wholesale supplier of
organically grown vegetables, fruit
and other produce. Supplies eighty
box schemes throughout the country
– contact company and it will put you
in touch with your nearest box scheme
or mail order supplier.

Eggs and dairy:
See also: *Farmers' Markets and Farm
Shops; Meat, Poultry and Fish; Home
Delivery Organic Supermarkets*

Green & Black's
P. O. Box 1937,
London W11 1ZU
Tel: 020 7633 5900
Fax: 020 7633 5901
E: enquiries@wholearthfoods.co.uk
W: www.wholeearthfoods.co.uk

Award-winning quality organic
chocolate. Increasingly widely available
at supermarkets as well as healthfood
stores nationwide.

Rachel's Organic Dairy
Unit 63, Glanyrafon Industrial Estate,
Aberystwyth SY23 2AE
Tel: 01970 625805
Fax: 01970 626591
E: enqs@rachelsdairy.co.uk
W: www.rachelsdairy.co.uk

Dairy products made solely from fresh
milk, organic fruit, organic sugar and
live cultures. Supplies a wide range of
wholesalers, supermarkets and
individual retailers nationwide.

**Rocombe Farm Fresh
Ice Cream Ltd**
Old Newton Road, Heathfield,
Newton Abbot TQ12 6RA
Tel: 01626 834545
Fax: 01626 853777
E: rocombe@globalnet.co.uk
W: www.rocombefarm.co.uk

Luxury organic dairy ice cream, frozen
yogurt and fruit sorbet. Available in
many independent retailers throughout
the country, also some supermarkets.

Meat, poultry and fish:

Eastbrook Farm Organic Meat

Eastbrook Farm, Bishopstone,
Swindon, Wilts SN6 8PW
Tel: 01793 790 460
Fax: 01793 791 239
E: info@helenbrowningorganics.co.uk
W: www.helenbrowningorganics.co.uk

Supplies a full range of fresh organic meat, bacon, cured ham and sausages nationwide to retailers, the catering trade and direct to consumers through their home delivery service.

Graig Farm Organics

Dolau, Llandrindod Wells, Powys
Tel: 01597 851655
Fax: 01597 851991
E: sales@graigfarm.co.uk
W: www.graigfarm.co.uk

Extensive range of organic meats, including specialities such as Welsh Mountain mutton, fish and pies. Mail-order service also includes a range of other organic produce, including dairy products, bread, groceries, fruit and vegetables, alcoholic drinks and non-food items, including skincare and books, plus organic woollens from farm's own sheep.

Longwood Farm

Tuddenham St Mary,
Bury St Edmunds IP28 6TB
Tel/Fax: 01638 717 120
W: www.longwoodfarm.co.uk

Specialist organic meat producer, retailer of fine organic foods – meat, dairy, cheese and provisions. Huge range of over 2,000 items. Nationwide plus local deliveries.

Organic Meat Matters

2 Blandys Farm Cottage, Letcombe Regis, Wantage OX12 9LJ
Tel: 0800 067 426/01235 762461
Fax: 01235 772526

Delivers fresh organic poultry, meat and fish, as well as eggs, fruit and vegetables and groceries to over 3,000 customers throughout the UK. Other meat products include organic sausages, burgers, pâtés and pies.

Swaddles Green Farm

Hare Lane, Buckland St Mary,
Chard TA20 3JR
Tel: 01460 234387
Fax: 01460 234591
E: information@swaddles.co.uk
W: www.swaddles.co.uk

Specializes in home delivery of award-winning organic meat, pies, bacon, hams, ready cooked meals, pâté etc. Also supplies groceries, dairy produce, children's food, alcoholic and non-alcoholic drinks.

Flour and baked goods:

Doves Farm Foods Ltd

Salisbury Road, Hungerford,
Berks RG17 0RF
Tel: 01488 684 880
Fax: 01488 688 235
E: mail@dovesfarm.co.uk
W: www.dovesfarm.co.uk

Manufacturer of a wide range of gourmet flours, cereal, biscuits, bread and cakes.

Little Watermill

Little Salkeld, Penrith,
Cumbria CA10 1NN
Tel: 01768 881523

Working traditional watermill producing a range of organic and biodynamic flours. Mail-order service available for a range of flours, dried fruit, nuts, pasta, tea, coffee etc.

The Village Bakery

Malmerby, Penrith, Cumbria CA10 1HE
Tel: 01768 881515
Fax: 01768 881848
E: info@village-bakery.com
W: www.village-bakery.com

Supplier of an extensive range of organic bread and cakes, hand-baked in wood-fired brick ovens, as well as jams and preserves, flours and baking sundries. Mail order, also run bread-making courses.

Family Matters

Organizations:

The Active Birth Centre

25 Bickerton Road, London N19 5JT
Tel: 020 7561 9006
Fax: 020 7561 9007
E: mail@activebirthcentre.com
W: www.activebirthcentre.com

Offers information and support and runs informative courses for the full range of childbirth options, including yoga for pregnancy and baby massage.

Baby Milk Action
23 St Andrews Street,
Cambridge, Cambs CB2 3AX
Tel: 01223 464420
Fax: 01223 464417
E: info@babymilkaction.org
W: www.babymilkaction.org

Non-profit organization working within a global network, which aims to end the suffering caused by inappropriate infant feeding and to strengthen controls on the marketing of the baby food industry.

La Leche League (UK)
P. O. Box 3424, London WC1N 3XX
Tel: 020 7242 1278
W: www.stargate.co.uk/lllgb

Voluntary organization providing breastfeeding help and information, primarily through mother-to-mother support in local groups. Bi-monthly newsletter and 24-hour telephone helpline.

National Childbirth Trust
Alexandra House, Oldham Terrace,
London W3 6NH
Tel: 020 8992 8637
Fax: 020 8992 5929
W: www.nct-online.org

Charity offering information and support in pregnancy, childbirth and early parenthood, aiming to give parents the chance to make informed choices.

National Association of Nappy Services (NANS)
St George's House, Hill Road,
Birmingham B5 4AN
Tel: 0121 693 4649

Group connecting parents with local nappy washing services in their area. Contact it for details of local services.

Real Nappy Association
P. O. Box 3704, London SE26 4RX
Tel: 020 8299 4519
E: nappies@gn.apc.org
W: www.realnappy.com

Central source of information and advice on nappy-related issues. Contact association for a list of all reusable nappy suppliers.

Baby Products Suppliers:
Bambino Mio
50 Cedar Road, Northampton NN1 4RW
Tel: 01604 458 999
Fax: 01604 474 344
E: bambino@skynet.co.uk

Mail-order supplier of 100 per cent pure cotton pinless nappies, velcro-closing outer covers and accessories. Write or call for free brochure.

Cuddlebabes
22 The Stray, South Cave,
East Yorkshire HU15 2AL
Tel: 01430 425257
Fax: 0870 052 2499
E: enquiries@cuddlebabes.co.uk
W: www.cuddlebabes.co.uk

Full range of nappy products, as well as a range of baby clothing, toys, skincare, pushchairs, nursing bras and sanitary protection.

Earthwise Baby Ltd
P. O. Box 1708, Aspley Guise,
Milton Keynes MK17 8YA
Tel: 01908 585275
Fax: 01908 585771
E: internetenquiries@earthwisebaby.com
W: www.earthwisebaby.com

Wide range of nappies and acces-sories, as well as clothing, prams and buggies, nursing and maternity bras, sanitary protection, homeopathic birth kits and relaxation music.

EcoClothworks
144 Woodvale, London SE23 3EB
Tel: 020 8299 1619
Fax: 020 8299 6997
E: clothworks@hotmail.com
W: www.clothworks.co.uk

Offers a range of baby products, including organic cotton, shaped nappies with button fastening or shaped nappies in Jersey cotton with ties, clothes and bed linen.

Green Baby
345 Upper Street, Islington,
London N1 OPD
Tel: 020 7226 4345
Fax: 020 7226 9244
E: greenbabyco@hotmail.com
W: www.greenbabyco.com

Range of organic cotton nappies, accessories, baby skincare and health products.

Little Green Earthlets
Unit 1–3, Stream Farm, Chiddingly,
nr. Lewes, East Sussex BN8 6HG
Tel: 01825 873301
Fax: 01825 873303
E: sales@earthlets.co.uk
W: www.earthlets.co.uk

Supplies a range of organic cotton nappies, outer wraps and accessories.

Mothernature
Acorn House, Brixham Avenue,
Cheadle Hulme, Cheshire SK8 6JG
Tel: 0161 485 7359

Supplies breastfeeding accessories including an extensive range of nursing bras, breast pumps, books and leaflets.

The Natural Collection
Eco House, Monmouth Place,
Bath, BA1 2DQ
Tel: 01225 404 010/
Tel order line: 0870 331 33 33
Fax: 01225 469 673
E: sales@naturalcollection.com
W: www.naturalcollection.com

Vast range of children's and baby products, as well as home furnishings, clothing, food and drink, body care and even stationery available online or through mail-order catalogue. Delivery throughout the UK.

The Organic Baby Company
Units 39–40, The Enterprise Shopping Centre, Eastbourne, East Sussex
BN21 1BD

Tel: 01323 411515
Fax: 01323 442398
E: sales@theorganicbabyco.com
W: www.theorganicbabyco.com

Company dedicated to offering organic and natural products for your family – nappies and accessories, milks, toiletries, sanitary products and more.

Planet Vision
P. O. Box LB 764, London W1P 1HQ
Shop: 44 Parkway, London NW1 7AH
Tel: 020 7713 8202
W: www.planetvision.co.uk

Shop offering online and mail-order services. 100 per cent organic babies clothes as well as men's and women's clothes and accessories.

Sam I Am
4 Sharon Road,
Chiswick,
London W4 4PD
Tel: 020 8995 9204
E: Sam-I-Am@nappies.net
W: www.nappies.net
Supplies a range of organic cotton nappies and a range of pants, inserts, training pants and liners. Also supplies nursing bras.

Schmidt Natural Clothing
21 Post Horn Close,
Forest Row RH18 5DE
Tel/Fax: 01342 822169
E: glen@natural.swinternet.co.uk

Supplies a range of organic nappies and accessories. Also sells a range of clothing and bedding for babies, children and adults in organic and chemical-free cotton, wool and silk.

Spirit of Nature
Burrhart House,
Craddock Road,
Luton, Beds LU4 OJF
Tel: 0870 725 9885
Fax: 0870 725 9886
E: mail@spiritofnature.co.uk
W: www.spiritofnature.co.uk

Offers an extensive range of nappies and accessories, and also supplies a range of natural clothing, environ- mentally friendly household products and natural bodycare.

Baby Food:
Baby Organix
Freepost BH1 336, Christchurch,
Dorset BH23 2ZZ

Tel: 0800 393511
Fax: 01202 479712
W: www.babyorganix.co.uk

A huge range of babyfoods, which includes first foods from weaning and a range of baby and toddler snacks. Available from supermarkets, mail order, healthfood shops, Boots and other pharmacies and Mothercare. Check website for searchable list of stockists plus advice on weaning and recipes.

Babynat
SDF, 125 Parkway,
London NW1 1PS
Tel: 020 7380 0906

Baby foods from France, including a range of organic baby foods in jars with no added sugar, suitable for babies from weaning to one year, infant cereal, teething biscuits and formula milks. Available direct from Babynat and various mail-order companies.

Hipp
Nutrition advice line: 01635 528250.

German food company with a huge range of babyfoods suitable for babies from weaning to toddlers, as well as follow-on milks, drinks, desserts and yogurts and cereals. Available from supermarkets, healthfood shops and by mail order.

Holle
Haselor, College Road,
Bromsgrove, Worcs B60 2NF
Tel: 01527 832863
Fax: 01386 792622

Range of biodynamic wholegrain baby cereals and baby rusks. Available from healthfood shops or direct. Contact the company for suppliers.

Original Fresh Babyfood Company
Simply Organic, 20–21 Dryden Vale,
Bilston Glen, Midlothian, EH20 9HN
Tel: 0131 448 0440
Fax: 0131 448 0441
E: info@simplyorganic.co.uk
W: www.simplyorganic.co.uk

Fresh baby meals in pots that can be frozen, made by Simply Organic, a Scottish company set up by two mums. Available from supermarkets, Safeway, delicatessens and healthfood shops. Call the company direct for more information.

As Nature Intended

Health Organizations:
Aromatherapy Organisations Council
P. O. Box 19834, London SE25 6WF
Tel: 020 8251 7912
Fax: 020 8251 7942

UK governing body for aromatherapy – represents the majority of practising aromatherapists in the UK. Contact it to be put in touch with a properly qualified aromatherapist in your area and for information about training to become an aromatherapist.

Association of Reflexologists
27 Old Gloucester Street,
London WC1N 3XX
Tel: 0870 567 3320
E: aor@reflexology.org
W: www.reflexology.org

Largest independent reflexology organization in the UK, representing over 4,000 members nationwide. It sets the standards for reflexologists throughout the country. See its website or call for a list of accredited schools and professional practitioners in your area.

British Acupuncture Council
63 Jeddo Road,
London W12 9HQ
Tel: 020 8735 0400
Fax: 020 8735 0404
E: info@acupuncture.org.uk
W: www.acupuncture.org.uk

Register of fully qualified practitioners of traditional acupuncture with over 1,700 members. Call for free local lists.

British Complementary Medicine Association (BCMA)
249 Fosse Road South,
Leicester, Leics LE3 1AE
Tel: 0116 282 5511
Fax: 0116 282 5611
W: www.bcma.co.uk

An association representing nearly thirty complementary therapies and 26,000 practitioners throughout the UK. Contact it for a range of alternative therapists practising in your area.

British Herbal Medicine Association
Field House, Lye Hole Lane,
Redhill, Bristol BS18 7TB
Tel: 01453 751 389
Fax: 01934 863 472
W: www.ex.ac.uk/phytonet/bhma.html

Association that promotes use of herbal medicines and campaigns to make the treatments more widely available.

British Homeopathic Association
27a Devonshire Street,
London W1N 1RJ
Tel: 020 7935 2163
W: www.trusthomeopathy.org

Point of contact for homeopathic practitioners. Contact for a list of registered homeopathic doctors and vets.

British Massage Therapy Council
Greenbank House, 65a Adelphi Street,
Preston, Lancs PR1 7BH
Tel: 01772 881 063
W: www.bmtc.co.uk

Contact for a copy of the National Public register of qualified massage therapists and BMTC-accredited schools and organizations.

Institute for Complementary Medicine
P. O. Box 194, London SE16 7QZ
Tel: 020 7237 5165
Fax: 020 7237 5175
E: icm@icmedicine.co.uk
W: www.icmedicine.co.uk

Educational charity supporting the development of all forms of complementary medicine. This includes maintaining The British Register of Complementary Practitioners.

National Institute of Medical Herbalists
56 Longbrook Street, Exeter,
Devon EX4 6AH
Tel: 01392 426022
Fax: 01392 498963
W: www.btinternet.com/~nimh

Oldest body of practising medical herbalists in the world. Contact it for a list of fully qualified practitioners.

Natural Medicines Society
Market Chambers, 13a Market Place,
Derby, Derbys DE75 7AA
Tel: 01773 710002
Fax: 01773 533855
W: www.thenms.demon.co.uk

Consumer body that defends freedom of choice in medicine and works to protect and develop the availability of natural medicines and advance the practice of alternative and complementary medical treatments by promoting education, research and discussion.

Osteopathic Information Service
Room 432, Premier House,
10 Greycoat Place, London SW1P 1SB
Tel: 0118 951 2051
E: info@osteopathy.org.uk
W: www.osteopathy.org.uk

Contact for list of registered osteopaths near you, or check the website for advice and a searchable database.

Alternative Health Remedies:
Aromatherapy Supply Company
545 Wine Street, Bristol BS99 1NS
Tel: 0117 951 5270

Supplier to individuals, therapists and trade outlets of essential oils and other aromatherapy items. Call for brochure.

Neal's Yard (Natural Remedies) Ltd
Ingate Place, London SW8 3NS
Tel: 020 7627 1949
E: mail@nealsyardremedies.com
W: www.nealsyardremedies.com

Stockists of a wide range of herbs, essential oils and homeopathic remedies, plus a selection of natural skin and haircare products. Various London stores, also available via mail order.

ThinkNatural.com
Unit 7, River Park, Billet Lane,
Berkhamsted, Herts HP4 1HL
Tel: 0845 601 1223
W: www.ThinkNatural.com

Online natural health store. Supplies a wide range of products including vitamins and minerals, natural and homeopathic remedies, aromatherapy and natural bodycare, as well as an on-line newsletter.

Hair and Beauty:
Dr Hauschka Skin Care
c/o Elysia Natural Skin Care,
19/20 Stockwood Business Park,
Stockwood, nr. Redditch,
Worcester B96 6SX
Tel: 01386 792622
E: enquiries@drhauschka.co.uk
W: www.drhauschka.co.uk

Mail-order supplier of body and haircare preparations and make-up, hand-made to recipes developed in Germany in the 1950s. All herbs and plants used are grown biodynamically or organically. Call for a catalogue.

Eco-living

Organizations:
Association for Environment Conscious Building
Nant-y-Garreg Farm, Saron,
Llandysul, Dyfed SA44 5EJ
Tel: 01559 370908
E: buildgreen@aol.com

Promotes green building and has an extensive list of green suppliers and designers.

Ecological Design Association
The British School,
Slad Road, Stroud,
Gloucs GL5 1QW
Tel: 01453 765 575
Fax: 01453 759 211

Promotes awareness and practice of the design of products, systems and environments for healthy and sustainable living.

Energy Conservation:

Energy Efficiency Council

Tel: 01428 654 011

E: theceed@compuserve.com

Draught control and insulation advice
and information.

The Energy Saving Trust

21 Dartmouth Street,
London SW1H 9BP

Tel. 020 7222 0101

Fax: 020 7654 2444

E: info@est.co.uk

W: www.est.org.uk

Offers free independent advice to all
householders and small businesses on
energy conservation – how to reduce
fuel bills, how to get the best from your
appliances and so on. Grants available
to help cover costs.

National Energy Foundation

Tel: 0800 138 0889

W: www.natenergy.co.uk/
renewables.html

Free renewable energy advice.

Home Energy Efficiency Scheme

Energy Action Grants Agency,
Freepost, P. O. Box 130,
Newcastle-Upon-Tyne NE99 2RP

Tel: 0800 072 0150

Information on grants and assistance
available for draughtproofing, loft
insulation, cavity wall insulation and
heating controls for people aged over
sixty, on a low income, or on certain
types of benefit.

Energy Services Ltd

The Greenhouse Energy Centre,
35 Mill Street, St Peter Port,
Guernsey GY1 1HG

Tel: 01481 722299

Fax: 01481 722320

E: energy@itl.net

Nationwide specialist in energy
efficiency and renewable energy.
Supplies condensing boilers, solar
water heating systems, wind turbines
etc. and runs a consultancy service.

Wind and Solar Works

Solar Sense, The Environmental Centre,
Pier Street, Swansea SA1 1RY

Tel: 01792 371 690

Fax: 01792 371 390

Designs, supplies and installs a
comprehensive range of small- to
medium-scale renewable energy
equipment. Practical advice and
technical support offered to architects,
contractors and DIY installers.

Solar Trade Association

Tel: 01208 873 518

Advice on solar heating.

Natural DIY Products:

Auro

Unit 2, Pamphillions Farm,
Purton End, Debden, Saffron Walden,
Essex CB11 3JT

Tel: 01799 543077

Fax: 01799 542187

E: sales@auroorganic.co.uk

W: www.auroorganic.co.uk

Full range of organic paints in many
colours, varnishes, stains, waxes and
adhesives. All products made from
non-polluting materials with no
petrochemicals, biocides or fungicides
used. Mail order.

ECOS organic paints

c/o Lakeland Paints,
Unit 19 Lake District Business Park,

Kendal, Cumbria LA9 6NH

Tel: 01539 732866

Fax: 01539 734400

W: www.ecospaints.com

Environment Conscious Odourless
Solvent-free (ECOS) paints and
varnishes. Available in a range of
colours. Mail order only.

Nutshell Natural Paints

Hamlyn House, Mardle Way,
Buckfastleigh, Devon TQ11 0NR

Tel: 01364 642892

Fax: 01364 643888

Paints derived from natural raw materials, in traditional and bright modern
colours. Also supplies floor oil, floor
varnish, wax and Swedish floor soap.

Crucial Trading Ltd

79 Westbourne Park Road, London W2

Tel: 020 7221 9000

Fax: 020 7727 3634

E: sales@crucial-trading.com

W: www.crucial-trading.com

A wide range of natural floor coverings
including sisal, seagrass, coir, jute, wool
etc. Fittings throughout the UK. Call for
free samples and a catalogue.

Penrose Hardwood Flooring
The Woodland Centre, Whitesmith,
nr. Lewes, East Sussex BN8 6JB
Tel: 01825 872025
Fax: 01825 873060
E: pengroup.demon.co.uk

Hardwood and softwood flooring from
sustainable sources certified by the Soil
Association.

**Environmental Construction
Products**
26 Millmoor Road, Meltham,
Huddersfield, West Yorkshire
HD7 3JY
Tel: 01484 854898
Fax: 01484 854899

Specialist company offering range of
environmentally sensitive building
products. Mail order only.

Woodland Windows
Tel: 0161 480 0363

Produces ecologically sound building
products. Committed to using timber
that comes only from sustainable
sources and is certified by the Soil
Association.

**Household Cleaning
Products:**
See also: *Home Delivery Organic
Supermarkets*; *Baby Products
Suppliers*

The Little Green Shop
P. O. Box 2892, Brighton,
Sussex BN1 5QZ
Tel: 01273 508 126
Fax: 01273 506 723
Produces household cleaning products,
toiletries and cosmetics that are kind to
the environment and effective to use.
Call or write for a mail-order catalogue.

The Bio-D Company Ltd
64 St Nicholas Gate, Hedon,
Kingston-Upon-Hull
HU12 8HS
Tel: 01482 229950
Fax: 01482 229921

Household products made from
renewable resources, contain totally
biodegradable detergents, no
phosphates and no chlorine bleaches.
The range includes dishwasher liquid,
cleaners, spray polish, washing-up
liquid and more.

Fleur Aromatherapy
Pembroke Studios, Pembroke Road,
Muswell Hill, London N10 2JE
Tel: 020 8444 7424
Fax: 020 8444 0704
E: sales@fleur-aroma.demon.co.uk
W: www.fleur.co.uk

Supplier of a range of organic and
vegan aromatherapy skincare products.
Available from health shops, on-line
or by mail order.

The Green People,
Brighton Road, Handcross, Haywards
Heath, West Sussex RH17 6BZ
Tel: 01444 401444
Fax: 01444 401011
W: www.greenpeople.co.uk

Produces a range of products, all
based on pure organic herb and plant
materials. Available direct, through its
website or mail-order service, or from
health stores throughout the UK.

Grow Your Own

Information:
**Henry Doubleday Research
Association (HDRA)**
See: *Organizations*

Brogdale Horticultural Trust
Brogdale Road, Faversham,
Kent ME13 8XZ
Tel: 01795 535286
Fax: 01795 531710

Gardens:
Audley End Organic Kitchen Garden
Audley End House,
Saffron Walden,
Essex CB11 4JG
Tel: 01799 520444

Yalding Organic Gardens
Benover Road, Yalding,
nr. Maidstone, Kent ME18 6EX
Tel: 01622 814650

Suppliers:

The Organic Gardening Catalogue
Riverdene Business Park,
Molesey Road, Hersham,
Surrey KT12 4RG
Tel: 01932 253666
Fax: 01932 252707
Biological control and accessories:

Agralan
The Old Brickyard, Ashton Keynes,
Swindon, Wilts SN6 6QR
Tel: 01285 860015
Fax: 01285 860056

Defenders Ltd
Occupation Road, Wye,
Ashford, Kent TN25 5EN
Tel: 01233 813121
Fax: 01233 813633

Biowise
Hoyle Depot, Graffham,
Petworth, Sussex GU28 OLR
Tel/Fax: 01798 867574

Hurdles:
English Hurdle
Curload, Stoke St Gregory,
Taunton, Somerset TA3 6JD
Tel: 01823 698418
Fax: 01823 698859

Seed suppliers:
D.T. Brown & Co Ltd
Station Road,
Poulton-le-Fylde,
Lancs FY6 7HX
Tel: 01253 882371
Fax: 01253 890923

Mr Fothergill's Seeds
Gazeley Road, Kentford,
Newmarket,
Suffolk CB8 7QB
Tel: 01638 552512
Fax: 01638 750468

S.E. Marshall & Co Ltd
Regal Road, Wisbech,
Cambs PE13 2RF
Tel: 01945 583407
Fax: 01945 583407

Suttons
Woodview Road, Paignton,
Devon TQ4 7NG
Tel: 01803 696321
Fax: 01803 696321

Thompson & Morgan
Poplar Lane, Ipswich,
Suffolk IP8 3BU
Tel: 01473 688821
Fax: 01473 680199

Edwin Tucker & Sons Ltd
Brewery Meadow,
Stonepark, Ashburton,
Newton Abbot,
Devon TQ13 7DG
Tel: 01364 652403
Fax: 01364 654300

Unwins Seeds Ltd
Admail 324,
Cambridge CB4 9SE
Tel: 01945 588522
Fax: 01945 475255

Suppliers of wildflower
plants and seeds:
Emorsgate Seeds
Limes Farm, Tilney All Saints,
Kings Lynn, Norfolk PE34 4RT
Tel: 01553 829028
Fax: 01553 828803

John Chambers
15 Westleigh Road,
Barton Seagrave,
Kettering NN15 5AJ
Tel: 01933 652562
Fax: 01933 652576

The National Wildflower Centre
Court Hey Park,
Liverpool L16 3NA
Tel: 0151 7371819
Fax: 0151 737 1820

further reading

Why Organic?
Planet Organic: Organic Living, by Lynda Brown (Dorling Kindersley, 2000)

The Organic Directory, compiled by Clive Litchfield (Green Books, co-published with the Soil Association, 2000 – updated annually)

The Safe Shopper's Bible, by David Steinman & Samuel S. Epstein (Macmillan US, 1995)

Organic Living, by Michael van Straten (Frances Lincoln, 2001)

The Green Guide For London (Green Guide Publishing Ltd. 2000, updated annually)

Eating and Drinking
The Food Our Children Eat, by Joanna Blythman (Fourth Estate, 2000)

How to Avoid GM Food, by Joanna Blythman (Fourth Estate, 1999)

The Shopper's Guide to Organic Food, by Lynda Brown (Fourth Estate, 1998)

Family Organic Cookbook, by Carol Charlton (David & Charles, 2000)

Planet Organic: Organic Cookbook, by Renee J. Elliott & Eric Treuille (Dorling Kindersley, 2000)

Foods For Mind and Body, by Michael van Straten (HarperCollins, 1997)

The Healthy Food Directory, by Michael van Straten (Gill & Macmillan, 1999)

Superjuice, by Michael van Straten (Mitchell Beazley, 1999)

Planet Organic: Baby and Toddler Cookbook, by Lizzie Vann (Dorling Kindersley, 2000)

Organic Wine Guide, by Monty Waldin (Thorsons, 1999)

Family Matters
Active Birth: The New Approach to Giving Birth Naturally, Revised Editon, by Janet Balaskas (Harvard Common Press, 1992)

New Natural Pregnancy, by Janet Balaskas & Yehudi Gordon MD MRCOG (Gaia, 1998)

The NCT Book of Child Health, by Morag Martindale (Thorsons, 2000)

The Organic Baby Book, by Tanya Maxted-Frost (Green Books, 1999)

The NCT Complete Book of Babycare, edited by Daphne Metland (Thorsons, 1999)

The NCT Complete Book of Pregnancy, edited by Daphne Metland (Thorsons, 2000)

As Nature Intended
Planet Organic: Organic Beauty, by Josephine Fairley (Dorling Kindersley, 2001)

The Natural Health Bible, by Alan Stewart & Maryon Stewart (Vermillion, 2000)

Alternative Medicine: An Illustrated Encyclopaedia of Natural Healing (Element, 1999)

The Natural Home
The Healthy Home Handbook, by Alan Berman (Frances Lincoln, 2001)

Eco-Renovation, by Edward Harland (Green Books, 1999)

The New Natural House Book, by David Pearson (Gaia, 1998)

The Ecofriendly Home, by Dan Phillips (HarperCollins, 2000)

Grow Your Own
The Organic Gardener's Handbook, by Margaret Elphinstone and Julia Langley (Thorsons, 1995)

Organic Gardening for the 21st Century, by John Fedor (Frances Lincoln, 2001)

Bob Flowerdew's Organic Bible, by Bob Flowerdew (Kyle Cathie, 2001)

The Organic Garden Book, by Geoff Hamilton (Dorling Kindersley, 1987)

picture credits and acknowledgements

Authors: Chapters 1 and 2   Claire Clifton
Chapter 3   Jo Younger
Chapters 4 and 5   Mary Lambert
Chapter 6   Jane Eastoe
Editors: Charlie Ryrie and Jo Lethaby
Assistant Editor: Victoria Webb
Indexer: Sue Bosanko
Design: Liz Brown
Special Photography: Tim Imrie
Styling: Susan Downing

The Publishers would like to thank Sue Walker at Harvey Nichols for the kind loan of homeware and furniture (including designs by Emily Readett-Bayley) featured in the photography on pages 2, 8–9, 26–7, 28–9, 34–5, 88–9, 108–9,124–5 and 144–5. Sue Walker specialises in furniture made from recycled and sustainable materials, for more information contact her at Harvey Nichols, 109–125 Knightsbrige, London SW1X 7RJ, tel 020 7235 5000 (extension 2230) or fax 020 85713078.

Our grateful thanks also to Julie Ryan and the staff of Capel Manor Horicultural College in Enfield for their help and hospitality during photography.

Why Organic?
Good Housekeeping/National Magazine Company Limited:
4 Tom Leighton (rpt); 7 Sandra Lane (rpt); 14 Elizabeth Zeschin; 19 Hugh Johnson; 23 Elizabeth Zeschin; 24 Jean Cazals.
Other Sources:
1 HarperCollins/Tim Imrie; 8–9 HarperCollins/Tim Imrie; 11 Andy Collison/Anthony Blake Photo Library; 12 Timothy Dosogne/Image Bank; 17 Lisa J Goodman/Image Bank; 21 Claire Parker/Anthony Blake Photo Library.

Eating and Drinking
Good Housekeeping/National Magazine Company Limited:
31 Hugh Johnson; 32 Polly Wreford; 36 Colin Poole; 39 and 40 James Murphy; 43 Jean Cazals; 45 Laurie Evans; 46 Christopher Drake; 50 and 53 Jean Cazals; 54 Philip Webb; 59 Tom Leighton; 61 Elizabeth Zeschin; 63 Marie Louise Avory; 65 Elizabeth Zeschin; 66 Roger Stavell; 68 James Murphy; 71 Elizabeth Zeschin; 73 Jean Cazals; 75 Marie Louise Avory; 77 David Morris; 78 Roger Stavell; 81 Elizabeth Zeschin; 82 Good Housekeeping; 85 Jean Cazals; 86 Philip Webb.
Other Sources:
26–27 HarperCollins/Tim Imrie; 28–29 HarperCollins/Tim Imrie; 34–35 HarperCollins/Tim Imrie; 49 Sian Irvine/Anthony Blake Photo Library; 57 HarperCollins/Frank Wieder.

Family Matters
Good Housekeeping/National Magazine Company Limited:
95 Having a Baby/Nick Pope; 97 Having a Baby/Lisa Linder; 98 Having a Baby/Nick Pope; 101 Tom Leighton; 103 David Garcia.
Other Sources:
88–89 HarperCollins/Tim Imrie; 91 Rob Van Petten/Image Bank; 93 HarperCollins/Derek Lomas; 105 HarperCollins/Frank Wieder; 107 Marie O'Hara/The Garden Picture Library.

As Nature Intended
Good Housekeeping/National Magazine Company Limited:
111, 113 and 114 Roger Eaton; 119 Helen Marsden; 123 Hugh Johnson.
Other Sources:
108–109 HarperCollins/Tim Imrie; 116 Antony Edwards/Image Bank; 121 HarperCollins/Derek Lomas.

Eco-living
Good Housekeeping/National Magazine Company Limited:
127 Sandra Lane; 128 Lizzie Orme; 131 Tom Leighton; 132 Hugh Johnson; 135 Graham Atkins-Hughes; 137 Nick Carter; 139 Christopher Drake; 141 and 143 Lizzie Orme.
Other Sources:
124–125 HarperCollins/Tim Imrie.

Grow Your Own
Good Housekeeping/National Magazine Company Limited:
157 Jane Sebire; 158 Philip Webb; 170 Tom Leighton.
Other Sources:
144–145 HarperCollins/Tim Imrie; 146 and 149 Garden & Wildlife Matters; 151 A l Lord/The Garden Picture Library; 153 John Fetwell/Garden & Wildlife Matters; 154 Garden & Wildlife Matters; 161 Mayer/Lescanff/The Garden Picture Library; 162 Sam North/Garden & Wildlife Matters; 165 and 167 Garden & Wildlife Matters; 168 Lamontagne/Garden Picture Library; 173 Garden & Wildlife Matters.

Organic Directory
174–175 HarperCollins/Tim Imrie (rpts).

subject index

recipe index

recipe index